1986

N

THE **T***-FACTOR*

THE T-FACTOR

How To Understand Time and Use It Right

MARK L. STEIN, Ph.D.

Peter H. Wyden / Publisher

NEW YORK

Library of Congress Cataloging in Publication Data

Stein, Mark L
    The T-factor.

       1. Time—Psychological aspects. 2. Time allocation.
I. Title.
BF468.S64   158'.1   76-17275
ISBN 0-671-22407-7

Contents

Part One

THE T-FACTOR
IN YOUR LIFE

1

The T-Factor

For centuries, men and women have grappled with the mysteries of time. Artists, philosophers, and scientists portrayed, analyzed, and measured this invisible and elusive force of nature, largely without practical, rewarding results.

Today it is possible to focus on time from a fresh perspective, a viewpoint that promises to yield rich dividends in human satisfaction and well-being, the perspective of a new specialty: *time psychology*.

This book explores time as a crucial psychological force in your life, a source of power that you can harness to help you think more effectively, understand your emotions more clearly, and make important decisions more confidently.

We will also investigate the many ways in which time may become a negative influence in your life, a force that, when insufficiently appreciated or ignored, can cause you considerable discomfort—emotional and physical.

With the use of time psychology, time becomes a psychological atmosphere surrounding you as you go through life, a changeable climate that exerts an unseen yet highly potent influence on your feelings, thoughts, and behaviors.

Just as primitive man reacted emotionally to atmospheric

changes in temperature, humidity, and air pressure without understanding how these natural forces influenced him, modern man has, until recently, been unaware that he responds with great sensitivity to the *time atmosphere* that surrounds his life.

The psychology of time can help you understand the influence exerted by the time atmosphere and its highly charged impact on your own life. But what do we mean when we speak of time in the first place?

What Is Time?

Don't ask.

Although you're in good company if you do. Philosophers have given themselves, each other, and generations of philosophy students headaches by attempting to wrangle an answer out of the seemingly simple question of what exactly time *is*. Or whether there is such a thing as time at all. Or whether time has a beginning and an end. Or. . .

Those of us interested in the psychology of time are luckier than philosophers. We don't have to worry about the problem of pinning time down to an airtight definition. We have a different, more immediate, and, for practical everyday application, more interesting question to ask:

How can we understand the connection between time—whatever it may be—and our individual feelings and actions?

By asking the question this way we avoid becoming enmeshed in the cosmic PROBLEM OF TIME and can zero in on the down-to-earth matter of *time as we experience it.*

The difference between the psychological outlook on time taken in this book and the cosmic (sometimes comic) approach to time taken by philosophers comes across even in a brief look at the way philosophers and psychologists handle an old logical dilemma. To wit: Does a tree that crashes in the forest make a noise if no one is present to hear it fall?

Philosophers generally answer, "Yes and no." (They like to cover all the bases.) In objective terms, they say, the falling tree does make a noise, even if nobody hears it. But in subjective terms, they counter, only by hearing the noise can a person really be sure it exists.

Ask a psychologist the same question and he's likely to reply, "Who cares?" Since he is interested in what happens to people, he immediately loses interest if no one is present to hear the tree fall. But if a person is present and does hear the tree fall, the psychologist becomes quite interested indeed and begins to ask questions: What does the person do when he hears the noise? Does he run away? Does he feel afraid? Does he seek shelter behind a rock or in a hollow?

The psychologist, then, is interested in behavior, in how the person reacts to the noise. He becomes concerned with the noise itself only when it becomes a factor in the person's behavior, in his thoughts, feelings, and actions.

Psychologically speaking, something becomes a factor in your behavior when it exerts a definite effect on your actions. If a tree falls in a forest 2000 miles from where you are sitting right now, the noise it makes is not a factor in your behavior. It has no effect on you at all. But if you happen to be sitting under that tree at the moment it begins to fall, its noise will certainly exert a considerable effect on you. It becomes a definite factor in your behavior.

For most people, philosophical speculations about the nature of time are comparable to the sounds of trees falling in distant forests. These aspects of time are not factors in their behavior. Unfortunately, much of what has been written about time belongs in this category.

Psychologists have discovered a number of aspects of time that do exert a definite effect on the behavior of people in general and—as I'm about to show—on you in particular. And since time often can be a most powerful factor in your behavior, it will be useful to focus on the *time factor* (or *t-factor,* for short) in your life and steer clear of weighty philosophical questions that have no real effect on you.

Instead of asking what time is, you'd do better to ask: How does the t-factor in my life affect me? How can I use the t-factor to my advantage? And first of all: How *time-sensitive* am I?

Some people maintain a productive and rewarding relationship with the t-factor; others suffer the t-factor's negative effects. Dr. Robert Knapp, a Wesleyan University time psychologist, found through extensive research that people vary between two extremes in relation to the t-factor. At one extreme is the time servant, the person who experiences time as a taskmaster and an adversary. At the other extreme is the "time master," a person who seems to be at peace with the t-factor in his life.

Ask yourself the following questions, drawn from Dr. Knapp's research:

	YES	NO
1. Does it annoy you a great deal to find that your watch has stopped?	——	——
2. Do you feel extremely guilty if you sleep late in the morning?	——	——
3. Do you feel that you often waste time or spend it uselessly?	——	——
4. Do you feel anxious when you're not certain of what time it is?	——	——
5. Do you often make out written time schedules for yourself?	——	——
6. Do you feel very guilty when you are late for appointments?	——	——
7. Do you feel that you have too little leisure time?	——	——
8. Do you arrive for appointments at the last minute?	——	——

Add up your number of YES answers to obtain your time-sensitivity score. Roughly speaking, the more items you marked YES the more time-sensitive you are. If you responded positively to at least five of the questions, you react quite intensely to the t-factor in your life. Time is a source of pressure and concern for you, a swift treadmill, and you must hurry to keep pace with it.

If you answered YES to few or none of the items, this does not necessarily indicate that you enjoy mastery over time. A low score on this questionnaire may merely suggest that you are *time-oblivious* rather than time-sensitive, unaware of the influence time wields on your feelings and actions.

In a way, the time-oblivious person is less fortunate than the time-sensitive one. Since the first step in treating an ailment is to diagnose it properly, the time-sensitive person's awareness of his problems with the t-factor gives him a head start in solving them.

Of course, a simple eight-item checklist can barely skim the surface of your relationship with the t-factor. Your experience of time penetrates and colors many of the more subtle levels and layers of your personality that combine to make you the unique person that you are. In order to discover how the t-factor in your life affects you in a wide range of your activities, you have to do a bit of self-exploration, journeying inward in search of the impact that time exerts on the quality of your life. What would be more appropriate to carry you along during this inward journey than a *time machine?*

Meet Your Time Machine

Most people think of time machines as fantastic H. G. Wellsian contraptions used by science-fiction adventurers to wander through centuries of the distant past and remote future. Such a time machine is still nonexistent. But one type of time machine really does exist. In fact, four billion such devices are in operation—and you are one of them.

Picture your life as a long highway of time. You enter this highway from an access ramp marked BIRTH and, much later, leave it from an exit ramp marked DEATH. Your life consists of your journey through time between these two points along the highway.

When you travel along a real highway by automobile, you are riding in what may be called a space machine, a vehicle capable of traveling through miles of distance. In the same way, as you travel through days, months, and years along the imaginary highway of time, the vehicle that propels you may be considered a time machine. It consists of your body and your mind.

Your body literally carries you along the highway of time from birth to death. On this physical level, all human beings are *time travelers* and their bodies are time machines. But your body is an exceedingly slow time machine; it inches along the highway second by second. Must you be restricted to this slow, one-directional style of time travel?

Not at all. Your time machine is able to move quite rapidly on the highway of time—and in two directions: into the future when it is in forward gear and into the past when it is in reverse. Your mind provides the accelerator for this rapid travel. A few quick demonstrations will display the capacity of your time machine for rapid travel into the past and future.

To travel into the past, answer the following questions: Do you remember your first date? Your high school graduation? Your first day on your present job? The day men landed on the moon?

You probably do, thanks to your brain, that marvelous time machine that can carry you back to your past through the mechanisms of memory. An experiment conducted by Canadian neurologist Wilder Penfield provides dramatic proof that your brain can indeed function as a time machine to the past.

Dr. Penfield was interested in determining the effects of stimulating various regions on the brain's surface with small amounts of electricity. Employing a painless technique that allowed the patient to remain conscious during brain surgery, Dr. Penfield touched exposed portions of the brain with a thin, electrically-charged probe.

The results were remarkable. This patient, like many others that Penfield studied, responded to stimulation of certain brain areas by directly reexperiencing long-forgotten events that had occurred much earlier in his life. The experiences were vivid and clear. It was as though the patient, while still on the operating table, had traveled backward in time to an earlier point in his life and had relived events that previously seemed to have disappeared forever into the past.

Dr. Penfield's research confirmed the notion that the brain can function as a time machine, propelling us in reverse along the highway of time to events and experiences that took place much earlier. In Chapter 4, we will begin to make use of your ability to travel backward in time to investigate the effects that your own past exerts on your present life. You'll be happy to learn that instead of poking your brain with electric probes, I will use a psychological time-travel technique called *Landmark Analysis* to effect this backward journey.

Since time is a two-way street, the brain can also carry us to the future. You can demonstrate this for yourself by answering such questions as: What will tomorrow be like for me? Will it be a busy day, full of work, or will it be a day of rest and relaxation? How about next April? Will I be working on my income taxes?

You were probably able to answer these questions, and in doing so, you traveled into the future by means of an extremely valuable quality of your brain—your capacity for anticipation.

Research has revealed that human beings, unlike lower forms of life that are firmly rooted in the present, are capable of projecting themselves into future situations through the mechanisms of anticipation. Some popular and highly effective systems of psychotherapy make use of this uniquely human capacity, and in later chapters we'll consider how you might apply these methods to your own problems in living.

In Chapter 5, you will begin to learn a technique called *Target Age Analysis* which will enable you to discover the influence your personal future wields on your present life.

It is useful to think of yourself as a time machine capable of traveling to the past and to the future, because many of your problems in day-to-day living will leap into clear focus when you think of them as difficulties you encounter in navigating your time machine through the days and years of your life.

How to Use this Book

This book has been developed as an instruction manual, to assist you in the operation, care, and maintenance of your personal time machine so you will be time's master, not its slave. It is the equivalent of the manual you receive when you purchase a new car.

Most operating manuals begin with a section on the vehicle's dimensions, its weight, length, and mileage. So this operating manual starts with chapters on your time machine's three major dimensions: your psychological present, your psychological past, and your psychological future.

Since it is helpful in operating a machine to understand something about what makes it run, Part Two will focus on the mechanical aspects of your time machine: How your brain and body combine to form the engine, or pacemaker, that propels you through time.

Just as the driver of an automobile sometimes encounters poor riding conditions caused by inclement weather or bumpy roads, psychological hazards called *time traps* lie in the path of your time machine. We'll examine the six most important time traps in Chapters 11 through 13 and discover strategies for coping with the t-factor when it becomes a negative atmospheric force in your life.

More devastating and unavoidable than time traps are the dangerous intersections in time that you are certain to cross as you propel your time machine through life. These intersections, where the t-factor becomes a potentially explosive force in your life, are *time bombs*. Chapter 14 will map out the location of these bombs embedded in your highway of time and consider techniques for defusing them and controlling their disruptive forces.

When a machine is badly constructed, poorly maintained, or improperly fueled, it obviously is likely to malfunction seriously or break down completely. Your time machine is no exception, so Chapter 15 will consider a number of situations where the t-factor runs wild.

Sensible vehicle owners like to get as much use as possible out of a machine in the most efficient way and with the least possible waste. As the operator of your personal time machine, you probably share this objective, and Chapter 16 will offer suggestions for tuning your time machine so you may extract maximum benefits from the t-factor.

By then you should be a proficient operator of your time machine. If you have children, you might then be interested in offering them some guidance for dealing with the t-factor in their lives. Chapter 17 will enable you to understand the development of your child's relationship to the t-factor and help you assist him or her in forming a healthy partnership with time.

Your operating manual will conclude with some advice for steering your time machine into relatively uncharted territory —the future. Perhaps you have been one of the many people who focus on the *tyranny of time,* watching helplessly as the future sweeps over your life like an ocean eroding a beach. Chapter 18, in combination with all the preceding chapters, will offer you a new way of dealing with the future, a positive approach based on sound psychological principles.

After all, the future is the direction in which all our time machines are heading. Perhaps you anticipate a frightening journey in a vehicle that sometimes seems more or less out of control. Others feel able to steer their time machines skillfully down life's highway and as a result derive enormous enjoyment from the trip.

Time psychology, as I will demonstrate in this manual, can help make your own journey into the future a rewarding one.

2

Your Time Frame

Each of us has our own unique, individual way of experiencing time, determined by the dimensions of our time machine. These dimensions form a framework, comparable to the chassis of an automobile, a mental suspension system that cushions travel through time and determines the smoothness or bumpiness of our experiences with the t-factor.

Your *time frame* consists of your attitudes, perceptions, and feelings regarding time. Most people are unaware that they have a time frame; like the suspension of an automobile, it lies beneath the surface of the machine. Still fewer people have learned to use their time frames as tools for self-understanding. Fortunately, with some simple techniques you can develop a detailed description of your personal time frame and clarify your thinking about the t-factor in your life.

The most important feature of your time frame is that it consists of the three basic elements I have mentioned:

1. Your Psychological Present
2. Your Psychological Past
3. Your Psychological Future

We'll look at each of these components singly, but first it will be helpful to gain an overview of your time frame as a whole. The *time-line* method makes this possible.

The most useful way to visualize your time frame is to picture it as a straight line. To obtain a graphic image of your *universal time line,* imagine that this dotted line

. . . .

represents all the time that ever existed or will ever exist in the universe: The left edge of the line represents the beginning of time; the right edge represents the end.

Most people find it difficult to relate to the concept of universal time. The idea of eternity is too abstract, too distant from real life concerns. People seem so threatened by the idea of infinity that they attempt to cut it down to size through humor. A famous psychologist used to illustrate this by telling his students a story about a tailor who advertised "eternity trousers."

A customer bought a pair of these trousers, imagining that they would last forever. Their seat soon wore out, however, and the customer brought them back complaining that he had been cheated. The tailor ingeniously replied that eternity means "without end," and that, since the trousers were now in this condition, he had fulfilled his side of the bargain.

Eternity is so open-ended an idea that it becomes a psychological dead end. Only a much narrower band on the universal time line is relevant to your real experience of time.

When we magnify that portion of the universal time line that covers the years between 1900 and 2100, the resulting time line looks like this:

1900   2100

– – – – – – – – – – – – – – – –

Place the letter *A* at the approximate point along this time line that represents your year of birth, and the letter *Z* at the point representing your most likely time of death. If you were born in 1935, for example, and expect to live approximately 75 years, your time line looks like this:

1900   *A*   *Z*   2100

– – – – ———————————— – – – –

How difficult was it for you to locate the position of point Z on this time line?

Many people find it challenging and somewhat unnerving to think about the length of time they will live. While the average life expectancy for Americans born in this century ranges from about 60 to 75 years (with younger people enjoying, on average, the prospect of a longer life span), individual predictions of life length vary tremendously from person to person. The placement of point Z on the time line tells us how long a life you expect to have and, more significantly, how much more time you anticipate having at your disposal from today onward.

The portion on the above time line that lies to the left of point A represents your *historical past* and includes all the time that occurred before you were born. The portion to the right of point Z represents your *fictional future* and includes all the time that will exist after you cease to. Points A and Z are the outer limits of your personal time frame.

By drawing your time frame in this way, you also illustrate the first important lesson to be gleaned from it: In psychological terms, your experience of time is limited to the solid portion of the universal time line, the portion that represents the time that you experience directly.

While you might occasionally venture to the left of point A by studying the history of events that took place before you were born or travel beyond point Z by reading science-fiction accounts of events that will occur after your death, both these excursions are experienced only indirectly by means of imagination. It is the real time in your life, the time between points A and Z, that affects your thoughts, feelings, and behaviors.

When lifted from the universal time line, your personal time frame now looks like this:

A ————————————————————————————— *Z*

Between points *A* and *Z* lies all that is included in your direct experience of time. To locate your current position on your time frame, draw a small *p* (for present) to indicate the point in the time frame that represents your estimate of how far you've traveled up to now between *A* and *Z*.

Where did you place your *p?* Generally, people 35 or younger place the *p* to the left of center; the over-35s tend to feel that it belongs to the right of center.

With two further additions, your time frame will become complete. On the portion of the line between *A* and *p*, write the word *past;* on the section between *p* and *Z*, write the word *future.* Your time frame should now look like this:

A	past	*p*	future	*Z*

These are the dimensions of your time machine: your psychological present, your psychological past, and your psychological future. Each of these elements has great significance for your relationship with the t-factor in your life. Let's examine them one at a time.

3

Your Psychological Present

Your psychological present is your feeling of *nowness*. As you read this sentence, each word that your eyes sweep across exists in your psychological present at the precise instant you look at it: It is *now*—your psychological present.

Some time psychologists claim that, in a strict sense, your psychological present does not really exist. They think your feeling of nowness is an illusion and refer to this now feeling as the specious present, *specious* meaning false or illusory. William James, one of the first scientists interested in the psychology of time, said of the specious present: "Let anyone try to attend to the *present* moment of time. One of the most baffling experiences occurs. Where is it, this present? It has melted in our grasp, fled ere we could touch it, gone in the instant of becoming."

John E. Boodin, a student of William James, put the dilemma a bit more lightheartedly by imagining a conversation between a celestial visitor to earth who has just seen a clock and an earthling trying to explain it to him:

"Hello there," the alien says, "what's that?" And on being told that this is an instrument to measure time

with, he asks: "Well how much time is it?" He is told
that it is one hour and thirty minutes. "All right," he
says, "one hour and thirty minutes." "No," the terrestrial
being says, "it is now one hour, thirty minutes, and five
seconds." In blank astonishment the celestial replies:
"You say that it is one hour and thirty minutes and you
say it is one hour, thirty minutes, and five seconds.
Which do you want me to believe?" "No," the terrestrial
says, "it is one hour, thirty minutes, and thirty seconds."
"You are a liar!" says the celestial. "No," says the terrestrial, "look and see, it is just one hour and thirty-one
minutes." By this time the language of the celestial is not
such as ought to be heard by mortal man, and so we will
close the interview.

The concept of time frames illustrates what James Boodin
and like-minded scientists are talking about. The sectors representing your psychological past and future take up almost
all the frame, squeezing the psychological present between
them and dwarfing it by comparison. According to the
specious-present viewpoint, the present moment—your feeling of nowness—immediately disappears into the past as you
move into the future; you can never really capture your psychological present because it departs so quickly. If you look
at it this way, only by halting time in its tracks would it be
meaningful to speak of your psychological present.

Other psychologists feel that your psychological present is
spacious rather than specious because it encompasses your
past and your future. The branch of psychotherapy called
Gestalt therapy maintains that everybody lives only in the
here-and-now. Contained in our psychological present, according to the Gestalters, are our memories of the past and
our hopes and fears for the future. A time frame drawn according to Gestalt specifications would look like this:

(_ _ _ _ _ PRESENT _ _ _ _ _)

A   past   future   *Z*

So these are two extreme ways of thinking about your psychological present: your specious present fades away so quickly that it cannot be captured; your spacious present engulfs every moment of your life from birth to death.

Most people who are asked to define their psychological present steer a middle course between these two extremes. Some regard the current year as the psychological present; others feel more comfortable with the current month. Still others are less spacious and think of each day as their psychological present. Most frequently, though, it is the current week that forms the psychological present in most time frames, which then look like this:

A   past   /this week/   future   Z

In your time frame, the psychological present most likely is a band of seven days. Let's lift this section from your time frame, magnify it, and see how your psychological week interacts with the t-factor in your life.

Rating Each Day in Your Week

What do the days of the week mean to you in a psychological sense? Everyone has his own way of thinking about the week, and it reveals a good deal about his relationship with the t-factor.

You can rate the days of the week on a scale of one to seven in terms of how much you like or dislike each day. Assign a value of one to your favorite day, two to the day that occupies second place in your preferences, and so on; seven is assigned to your least favorite day.

DAY	RATING
SUNDAY	____
MONDAY	____

TUESDAY	——
WEDNESDAY	——
THURSDAY	——
FRIDAY	——
SATURDAY	——

Dr. Maurice Farber, a research psychologist at New York University, asked 80 research subjects to rate the days of the week in this way. When he averaged all their ratings, he found that his subjects had ranked the days of the week in this order, from most-favored to least-favored:

SATURDAY
FRIDAY
SUNDAY
THURSDAY
WEDNESDAY
TUESDAY
MONDAY

One striking—if hardly surprising—implication of Dr. Farber's findings was that the average psychological week of his subjects was divided into two distinct parts: the workweek (Monday through Thursday) and the extended weekend (Friday through Sunday). Obviously, Dr. Farber's subjects favored the weekend over the workweek in their attitudes toward the psychological present. Saturday, Friday, and Sunday received the highest ratings; the remaining four days were progressively less favored as they became more distant from the weekend. He felt that these results strongly indicated a powerful leisure-time orientation on the part of his subjects.

How did your own ratings compare to those reported by Dr. Farber's research subjects? Did they correspond precisely or was there wide divergence? In making these comparisons, it is important to remember that by averaging the 80 ratings together, individual differences between the present time frames of Dr. Farber's subjects became blurred. Most likely, at least some chose Monday as the most-favored day and relegated Saturday to last place.

If you'll examine your rating of the days of the week, you can obtain some insight into the psychological significance of the current week in your time frame.

What Does Sunday Mean to You?

While Sunday captured third place in Dr. Farber's research, it is a day that many people regard as their favorite. If you assigned first place to Sunday, you are leisure-oriented (assuming that you are not one of the few people who work on Sundays).

Some people, though, rate Sunday as one of their least-favored days. If you assigned a value of five, six, or seven to Sunday, you're a member of this group and, most probably, place a higher value on work and achievement than on leisure and relaxation.

Intensely work-oriented people often think of Sunday as an excruciatingly barren desert of closed offices, empty streets, and out-of-touch business associates separating them from the "real life" oasis of the workweek. For such individuals, time seems to come to a dead stop after sundown on Saturday and begins again only when the alarm clock rings on Monday morning. During the workweek, the t-factor remains in the background, operating beneath the level of their awareness. But on Sunday, the frenzy of work lifts like a curtain, leaving center stage to the t-factor for 24 long hours.

While most of us seem to value a work-free Sunday for its leisure activities, the Sunday haters think that a long afternoon of picnicking or football is a good way to do "nothing." There is even a psychiatric disorder associated with the stresses that Sundays hold for certain individuals. Dr. Sandor Ferenczi, a pioneer of psychoanalysis who practiced in Budapest, observed that many of his patients experienced painful bodily sensations, primarily headaches, almost every Sunday. Mysteriously, these patients felt fine during the balance of the week.

The Sunday Neurosis

Since no physical basis could be detected for his patients' pain, Ferenczi believed that they were symptoms of psychological distress and sought the roots of this ailment in careful psychoanalytic interviews. Ferenczi concluded that the cause of this weekly disorder, which he labeled the Sunday neurosis, could be traced to early childhood.

Many patients who suffered from Sunday neurosis reported that they had been severely punished in childhood when, as so many children do, they became carried away during Sunday outings and "ran wild" in a frenzy of pleasure. The experience of being punished for Sunday pleasures, according to Ferenczi, led these patients to associate rest and recreation with punishment.

Sunday, the day set specifically aside for rest and recreation, therefore reawakened such unpleasant associations each week even decades later and literally made Ferenczi's patients sick. In terms of time psychology, I would explain the Sunday neurosis by saying that the t-factor becomes a weekly negative force in the Sunday neurotic's life.

But you don't necessarily have to be a neurotic to dislike Sunday; traumatic childhood experiences are not the sole cause of a negative t-factor on the first day of each week. Perhaps your upbringing stressed the virtues of hard work, self-denial, and constant striving for success. If this is the case, you've probably been forced to suppress your natural hedonic drives—the urges for self-gratification and pleasure that all human beings share—by regarding them as wasteful, possibly sinful, certainly unwelcome.

Then, when lazy Sunday pops up as a distressingly empty page in your appointment book, you react to it like a teetotaler forced to attend a beer party. You feel out of place and displaced in time. Sunday occupies an unpleasant sector in the part of your time frame that is your psychological present. On Sunday, your t-factor becomes an adversary, a mocking temptress offering the forbidden fruits of recreation and relaxation. Just as the teetotaler often harbors a deep-seated desire to drink himself into oblivion, the hard-driving Sunday hater who ruins the family picnic by calling it a waste of time is battling to control his secret yearning to indulge himself in the taboo pleasures of indolence and idleness.

Rating Your Weekdays

If you assigned top rankings to Monday, Tuesday, and Wednesday, it is likely that you also tended to assign Sunday one of your lowest ratings. Monday, Tuesday, and Wednesday are the favorite days of action-oriented individuals. Monday is the cure for the Sunday neurosis.

Those who favor these three days tend to regard the workweek as their natural habitat. Each Monday morning becomes a kind of rebirth, awakening new possibilities for accomplishment and achievement. The rest of the week seems to wait in the wings, bursting with large chunks of the t-factor, blank slates waiting to be filled with the record of productive activities.

If you assigned higher ratings to Thursday through Saturday, you probably have great difficulty getting out of bed on Monday morning, unlike the Sunday hater who plunges into Monday like a prisoner released after a long confinement. It is also likely that you are one of the leisure-oriented individuals typified by Dr. Farber's research subjects.

The expression blue Monday aptly describes the feeling you experience at the beginning of each week. Your low ratings of Monday through Wednesday may thus reflect some degree of dissatisfaction with your work life. If you feel trapped in a repetitive nine-to-five routine five days a week, your weekend becomes a refuge, a hideaway from the unpleasant necessity of earning a living.

While the Sunday hater lives to work, people who have blue Mondays and assign high ratings to the end of the week generally feel they merely work to live. If this applies to you it may be helpful for you to assess your current work situation. Is there room for growth to a more satisfying level of employment? Should you invest some time to acquire improved skills?

Dr. Farber's research subjects, after all, were college students who could regard their blue Mondays as a temporary affliction and look forward to future improvement in their work lives. You, on the other hand, may have to take a more active role in removing the blueness from your Mondays, Tuesdays, and Wednesdays so that you can curtail your yearnings for weekend escape.

4

Your Psychological Past

Everybody lives in the psychological past. The present moment zips by so quickly that when we seem to experience an event right now, we are actually remembering an event that occurred a moment or two earlier.

Some psychologists illustrate this by suggesting that you picture your time frame like this:

A	me	I→		Z
PAST			FUTURE	

Your *I* is your psychological present, advancing moment by moment into the future; your *I* stands for your immediate experiences and sensations. As your *I* proceeds through time, it leaves behind an ever-growing bundle of experiences, perceptions, feelings, memories. This bundle is the *me* aspect of your life; it provides you with a feeling of continuity and the sense that you are a person with solid roots in the past.

Most humans are powerfully influenced by the psychological past, and psychologists interested in tracing the effects of this influence have divided this time period into three parts: the immediate past, and recent past, and the remote past.

The immediate psychological past—defined as your most recent 60 seconds of life—is necessary to your ability to function effectively. Imagine what would happen if you lacked awareness of your immediate past. You'd find yourself in the situation faced by the patient who went to his neurologist and complained:

"Doctor, my memory is shot. I can't remember a thing."

"How long have you had this problem?"

"What problem?"

Actually the loss of the immediate psychological past is no laughing matter. Doctors most often encounter such a lack of the immediate past in patients with severe brain disease, often associated with a long history of alcoholism. When you recall that awareness of what is happening in one's daily activities is based completely on the ability to tune into the immediate psychological past, it becomes clear how devastating the loss of this small bit of the time frame can be.

The recent psychological past extends backward along your time frame from the present to about a week or so ago. The firmer your grasp of your recent past, the more able you are to cope with the demands of daily living. I know of a businessman who was having trouble with his grasp of the recent psychological past. He kept telephoning the same sales prospect at hourly intervals because he truly could not remember having made the previous calls.

A more common example of difficulty with the recent past is the phenomenon of name-forgetting. You meet a person at a cocktail party and exchange names. If you were asked the person's name after thirty seconds, you'd probably still remember it; your immediate psychological past would have captured the name. But two hours later, you might see the person again and not have the faintest notion of his name. It has escaped the grasp of your recent psychological past.

It is the remote psychological past, extending from about a week ago to the beginning of your conscious life, that accounts for much of your relationship to the t-factor. Some psychologists, in fact, take the extreme position that character and personality are totally distilled in the crucible of the first years of life, the remotest sector of your time frame. While this is debatable—and interminably debated—there is no doubt that one's present and future is potently shaped and influenced by the remote psychological past.

To investigate the quality of your psychological past, I will employ the Landmark Analysis technique, an analysis of psychological landmarks. The term *landmark* has been borrowed from pediatrics. Pediatricians use this word to identify successive steps in a baby's development in the early years of life. The child's first word, first attempt at crawling, first step, first exercise of bladder control are all landmarks along his road of development. Pediatric landmarks are thus events with great significance to a child's physical maturation.

Similarly, psychological landmarks are events located in your psychological past, though not necessarily in your childhood, that stand out with great force and clarity from the millions of events that you have experienced. Landmark Analysis investigates these significant standout events to determine the quality of your psychological past.

Perform Your Own Landmark Analysis

To set up your own Landmark Analysis, choose three events in your life, three occasions or experiences that had an unusual impact on you. You might, for instance, select your wedding day, an important birthday, or, as many research subjects do, that day in late November 1963 when President Kennedy was assassinated.

List the landmarks on the chart below, in chronological order, starting with the earliest:

AGE   LANDMARK

(1)
(2)
(3)

It may be helpful for you to examine, as an example, the following landmark list, produced by a 39-year-old female research subject:

	AGE	LANDMARK
(1)	16	Sweet sixteen party
(2)	22	Birth of first child
(3)	37	Fifteenth wedding anniversary

What can analysis of these landmarks tell us about this person? You've probably already come up with some reasonable speculations. It is apparent that she seems deeply involved with her sex role as a woman. Her landmarks all reflect a preoccupation with feminine concerns, from the ritualistic entry into womanhood at age 16 through fulfillment of the female biological function of childbirth at 22 to the marking of a decade and a half of domesticity at age 37.

A pervasive theme of femininity runs through this person's landmarks. It is possible, though not likely, that in addition to being a woman, wife, and mother, she is also a lawyer, secretary, or research physicist. But her Landmark Analysis is evidence that—regardless of her other life interests—the persistent theme of her psychological past is one of highly valued femininity, not vocational achievement or personal independence. Her psychological past seems to revolve exclusively about her family and her role as a woman; the outside world does not seem to intrude at all.

Now consider this Landmark Analysis, prepared by a 45-year-old man:

	AGE	LANDMARK
(1)	15	Parents killed in accident
(2)	20	Apprenticed to printer
(3)	34	Opened my printing business

We can safely deduce from this landmark list that the theme of this individual's psychological past is that of an independent struggle for success. His parents' death when he was 15 left him on his own, and his subsequent landmarks both relate to the achievement of success through hard work.

What is the theme of your Landmark Analysis? It may not leap out as plainly as the themes in my examples, but most landmark lists do reflect a theme.

The following questions are designed to help you discover whether your psychological past contains one of five major landmark themes:

1. Do your landmarks carry the theme of *achievement?* Events dealing with graduation, business success, athletic prizes, etc., qualify for this theme.

2. Do your landmarks suggest the theme of *passivity?* This may be true if you listed events that happened to you, for example: receiving a large inheritance, winning a lottery, being drafted, being promoted for seniority rather than merit.

3. Do your landmarks reflect the theme of *independence?* Events that you carried out by yourself, the fruits of your own exclusive efforts, suggest this theme.

4. Do your landmarks imply that *resentment* is the prominent theme in your psychological past? Resentment may be indicated if you listed events relating to being double-crossed, swindled, two-timed, etc.

5. Do your landmarks suggest the theme of *adversity,* such as bankruptcy, the death of a loved one, wartime injury, or the stock-market crash.

Your Landmark Analysis should provide you with a sharp insight into the nature of your psychological past. Since you had the freedom to select three events from the multitude of your experiences, it is clear that the theme conveyed by these events has a significant bearing upon the sort of person you have become.

It might now be apparent to you, for example, that your psychological past has been marred by the theme of resent-

ment, that too much of your time and attention were diverted
to the nursing of a grudge. Or the analysis may highlight that
you've allowed past adversities to dominate your subsequent
activities to an excessive degree. Is it time to stop licking your
wounds and return to battle?

Perhaps you will be pleased by the theme that emerged
from your analysis. Many people are. But, as we have seen,
your Landmark Analysis might well have brought into clear
focus some of your discontents with the quality of your past
relationship with the t-factor.

Our first research subject reacted with dissatisfaction to the
theme revealed by her Landmark Analysis. She felt that it
underlined how exclusively her psychological past revolved
about home and hearth. The analysis allowed her to realize
for the first time how little she had experienced of the world
outside her home. Spurred by the Landmark Analysis, she
embarked on constructive moves toward increased independence while preserving her still highly-valued family life.

Hopefully, the Landmark Analysis can perform a similar
service for you. If so, you will have begun to make constructive use of your psychological past.

5

Your Psychological Future

While your psychological future—the sector of your time frame from the present moment to the end of your life—strongly depends on the contents of your psychological past and present, it is still possible for you to influence and improve your future relationship to the t-factor.

The key to influencing the quality of your psychological future is your capacity for anticipation. With the assistance of the technique called Target Age Analysis, your ability to anticipate can be molded into a powerful tool for self-help.

Imagine lacking the capacity to anticipate the future. Without this skill, the simple act of walking down a flight of stairs would become a monumental task: Since you would not be able to anticipate the position of each successive step, you'd have to proceed slowly and carefully, looking at each step on your descent.

If you couldn't anticipate events, you'd be hungry and homeless. You know that you'll need money to buy food and pay rent next month, so you work for it this month. You know that you'll continue to need food and shelter after you retire, so you arrange a pension plan. How do you know things that have not yet occurred? You know them through the mechanisms of anticipation.

My examples relate to short-term anticipation—the next step on the staircase, next month's bills, etc. But the bulk of the future sector of your time frame is rather remote from the present moment and much more difficult to anticipate. This is why Target Age Analysis becomes useful.

Target Age Analysis is a refinement of a technique called future autobiography developed in the 1930s by a psychologist named Norman Israeli. Dr. Israeli established a branch of psychology called futurism and was mainly concerned with investigating the future time frames of psychologically abnormal individuals, patients in mental hospitals and clinics.

Israeli instructed the individuals he chose for study to imagine they had traveled a decade or two forward in time and to write an autobiography recounting the events that had occurred in the intervening years. Some of his research subjects produced massive future autobiographies tens of thousands of words in length. Target Age Analysis is a shorthand method of producing a much more succinct future autobiography.

How to Perform Your Target Age Analysis

To begin your Target Age Analysis, add ten years to your current age and record the result below:

_____ plus 10 years = _____
current age   target age

If you are currently 36 years old, then, your target age for this analysis is 46. Now, in the space provided, list three target objectives or goals that you wish to accomplish and feel capable of accomplishing by the time you reach your target age:

Objectives for _____
target age

(1)
(2)
(3)

Example: An 18-year-old male high school senior, whose target age was 28, listed these target objectives:

(1) Complete medical school
(2) Travel through Europe
(3) Remain single

Once you've listed your own target age objectives, the next step is to imagine that you have reached your target age and have, indeed, accomplished your three goals. In the space below, using your ability to anticipate, briefly describe what you picture your life to be like at your target age.

_____

_____

_____

_____

_____

The 18-year-old high school senior described his life at the target age of 28 in this way:

> I'm in my second year of residency at a big city hospital. New York or Chicago. Studying surgery and becoming very skillful with my hands. My social life is limited because of the time I spend studying or on call. I'm often lonely and regret not having gotten married. I look forward to my vacations and plan to revisit places I traveled to during my trip to Europe after college.

This small slice of future autobiography expresses some degree of dissatisfaction with this man's life at age 28. Does your own future autobiographical sketch reflect similar anticipated discontents?

If so, it may be useful for you to reexamine your target goals. Just as the Landmark Analysis of your psychological past might have suggested destructive themes in your life up to now, your target goals for the future may indicate the operation of destructive or negative values in your plans for the future. Such values usually lie beneath the level of your everyday awareness, yet they exert a powerful influence on those of your feelings and behaviors that are aimed at the future.

Your Target Age Analysis should enable you to review in advance the effects that the pursuit of such values will exert on the quality of your psychological future; it creates the opportunity to plan for your future in psychologically sound style.

6

Your Time-Frame Orientation

Since each of us has a time frame composed of the same three elements—psychological present, psychological past, and psychological future—all time frames are similar to some extent. But there also seem to be powerful differences between our individual time frames based upon the relative impact of each time-frame element upon our lives. Some of us seem to be dominated by the psychological past; others are firmly rooted in the psychological present; still others seem to live primarily in the psychological future.

To discover the relative importance of each of these time-frame elements, Dr. Norman Israeli asked a group of 607 research subjects the following six questions. How would you answer them?

	YES	NO
1. Do you consider your past to be more important than your future?	———	———
2. Do you consider your past to be more important than your present?	———	———

3. Do you consider your present to be more important than your past?   _____   _____

4. Do you consider your present to be more important than your future?   _____   _____

5. Do you consider your future to be more important than your past?   _____   _____

6. Do you consider your future to be more important than your present?   _____   _____

Your answers to these questions will provide you with a rough idea of your time-frame orientation. You are present-oriented if your response to questions 3 and 4 was YES and your response to questions 2 and 6 was NO.

If you answered YES to questions 1 and 2 and answered NO to questions 3 and 5, you may consider yourself past-oriented.

The future element of your time frame is predominate if questions 5 and 6 elicited a YES response from you while questions 1 and 4 drew a NO.

While this method of determining your time-frame orientation is somewhat crude, it does illustrate the broad outlines of your dominant time-frame elements.

Dr. Israeli found that his 607 subjects—college freshmen and sophomores—were rather present-oriented. Only 5 percent of his subjects considered the past more important than the present; a mere 6 percent regarded it as more important than the future; 93 percent considered the present more important than the past and 92 percent considered the future more important than the past.

There was less agreement regarding the relative importance of the present and future: 58 percent considered the present more important and 36 percent regarded the future more important. Statistically, Dr. Israeli's subjects rated the present 12 times as important as the past and 1.2 times as important as the future.

Further studies by a team of three researchers—Harriet Mann, Miriam Siegler, and Humphrey Osmond—revealed an important connection between time-frame orientation and personality.

The researchers divided people into four fundamental personality types, following a classification method originally developed by Carl Jung: *sensation type; feeling type; intuitive type;* and *thinking type.*

They found that each of these four personality types has a distinctive time-frame orientation. The sensation type (or *s-type*) is oriented toward the psychological present; the feeling type (or *f-type*) is oriented toward the psychological past; the intuitive type (or *i-type*) is oriented toward the psychological future; and the thinking type (or *t-type*) partakes of all three time-frame orientations.

We'll examine these four types of personality individually. You'll probably find that at least one of them meshes closely with your own personality features which will enable you to pinpoint your own particular time-frame orientation.

Are You the Sensation Type?

For the sensation type, life is a series of happenings that take place in the right-now. The s-type craves immediate gratification for his needs and desires and has difficulty with situations that require delay or patience. He does not experience time as a steady flow from past to future; he lives for the present moment. He is so exquisitely immersed in the psychological present that he feels little if any link with his own past or future. He is notoriously poor at waiting his turn. He wants what he wants when he wants it. He is constantly in motion, searching for an immediate influx of sensations and experiences. The s-type is at his best in a crisis or emergency. And because he dislikes planning for the future and seems incapable of learning from the past, he often does find himself in a crisis situation.

If this description corresponds to your own personality style, your time-frame orientation lies squarely in the psychological present. As a sensation type, you lead a hectic life, full of peaks (when your needs are gratified) and valleys (when you are forced to wait). You are vulnerable to two dangerous time traps—impulsivity and boredom—that will be fully described in Chapter 12.

Are You the Feeling Type?

The feeling type is most responsive to his psychological past. Even when very young, the f-type filters his current experiences through the sieve of memory and reminiscence. Others therefore regard him as sentimental. He seems incapable of behaving spontaneously in the present and feels comfortable only with long-established routines. The feeling type neither expresses a sense of urgency about getting things done quickly nor does he concern himself with solving a currently pressing problem. He is more likely to confine himself to speculations over what led up to the problem in the first place.

The f-type is often preoccupied with sorting out his personal relationships; he may brood endlessly over past insults and grievances. Some cultural groups seem particularly prone to producing f-type individuals. The ancestor-worshipping Chinese, who emphasize the primacy of ancient social customs, are examples of one such f-type society. From another part of the world, Dr. Edward Hall, a cultural anthropologist, recounts an incident that occurred on the South Pacific island of Truk; it demonstrates how all-pervasive the past time-frame orientation can become. According to Dr. Hall, a Truk islander came to the police in a highly agitated state, reporting that a murder had occurred. Upon investigation, the police confirmed that a murder had indeed been committed—20 years earlier. To the f-type islander, the bloody event seemed as immediate as though it had taken place that very day.

While you are presumably not nearly as rooted in the psychological past as this Truk islander, the general description of the feeling type may fit your concept of yourself. If so, your time-frame orientation is toward the psychological past, and the time traps of nostalgia and depression lie in the path of your time machine. Chapter 11 will help you avoid them.

Are You the Intuitive Type?

To the intuitive type, life is pregnant with future possibilities and potentialities, at the expense of both current concerns and attention to the events of the past. For the i-type, time seems to flow too slowly; he is always racing toward a brighter tomorrow. While the sensation type might derive pleasure from the thrilling and immediate risk of gambling at the roulette wheel, the intuitive type is more inclined to invest in a promising though shaky business enterprise. He is regarded by others as something of a dreamer, because he engages in disorganized planning without spending sufficient time preparing a solid foundation for his schemes. He may be the idea man in a business, leaving the task of implementing his ideas to sensation types and the chore of keeping records to feeling types.

Occasionally, an intuitive type inspires many others with his utopian visions and becomes a charismatic leader, wielding great influence. The i-type is rarely satisfied with things as they are and is most comfortable when spinning rosy visions of things as he hopes they will be.

If the description of the intuitive type meshes with your own personality trends, your time frame is oriented toward the future. The time traps of anxiety and fantasy, as discussed in Chapter 13, pose real dangers for you.

Are You the Thinking Type?

The thinking type is equally oriented to all three of his time-frame elements. Continuity and logic are the basic themes of his personality. The t-type is a planner and an organizer, able to base his present actions on the lessons of the past and the portents of the future. He lacks the emotional vulnerability of the feeling type, the volatility of the sensation type, and the contagious enthusiasm of the intuitive type. He may therefore seem somewhat cold and detached. But because he has a keen awareness of the past, present, and future elements of his personality, he is capable of dealing effectively with a range of problems and challenges.

If your personality fits the description of the t-type, your orientation to all three of your time-frame elements is rather evenly balanced. Events that do not succumb to your talents for logic and organization, however, might well render you vulnerable to any of the time traps discussed in Chapters 11 through 13.

It will now be useful to examine the engine of your time machine—your psychological pacemaker—and see how it works.

Part Two

YOUR SENSE
OF TIME

7

Your Mind, Your Body, and Your Psychological Pacemaker

Time psychologists have long been interested in discovering the mechanisms underlying our experience of time. Is there a physical organ of time in the body, they ask, a time sensor comparable to the sense organs of vision and hearing? Or is the ability to perceive the flow and duration of time basically a mental process by which minds somehow classify experiences into the psychological present, past, and future?

These questions are a modern way of stating an age-old problem: What is the basis of our psychological experiences —the body or the mind?

The mind–body dilemma plagued psychology for generations, splitting psychologists into two warring camps. Some believed that all psychological experiences, including the sense of time, could be reduced to basic biological processes. This viewpoint was called the nothing-but school of psychology, since it was given to making pronouncements like: "Feelings of depression are nothing but chemical reactions that occur in the brain."

Other psychologists quarreled with this notion and adopted the something-more attitude. According to this view, men and women are something more than mechanical flesh-and-blood contraptions. Feelings of depression, they asserted, are something more than merely chemical reactions in the brain: they are human reactions to human problems.

A truce finally settled over this intellectual battlefield. The terms of the armistice were that psychological experiences would be looked at in two ways: as the result both of biological processes and of mental processes that could not yet be reduced to specific chemical reactions or nervous impulses.

This was really a way of saying that the mind and the body are two aspects of the same thing. Some psychologists concentrated on the biological basis of psychological experiences, others on the more mental aspects. Time psychology's search for the basis of our sense of time—our psychological pacemaker—has therefore followed these two pathways. Some time psychologists have sought the psychological pacemaker through investigating biological processes, others took the mental-process route. Since both explorations yielded information helpful in understanding the t-factor, we will examine your psychological pacemaker as a biological as well as mental piece of equipment.

8

Your Biological Pacemaker

Time psychologists who followed the biological route believe that bodily rhythms are the basis for our experience of the t-factor. Your body, they suggest, may be something of a biological clock.

This may seem a strange notion to those who believe that a clock must be a device with a second hand, minute hand, and hour hand. Actually, the clock that hangs on your wall is only one of many possible types of timepieces. Scientists define a clock as anything in nature that follows a definite, repetitive rhythm. A faucet that drips water so that each drop hits the sink at three-second intervals is a kind of clock. The unit of time for this faucet clock is the time that elapses between each falling drop. If you want to cook a three-minute egg, for example, but don't have a conventional timer handy, you could cook the egg until 60 drops of water had fallen. Since each drop falls at three-second intervals, 60 drops will fall in 180 seconds, which equal three minutes.

The essence of a clock, then, is rhythmic repetition. Since the human body is subject to a number of biological processes that follow regular and repetitive rhythms, scientists have wondered whether it is these clocklike processes that enable us to maintain a sense of time. One reason for their interest in this biological-clock idea is evidence that organisms can sense time with a great degree of accuracy without the use of mechanical timekeeping devices.

Many researchers have observed that animals possess what seems to be a natural ability to measure the passage of time. In a famous learning experiment, dogs were conditioned to salivate at the sound of a bell by being given food whenever the bell rang. The bell rang at five-minute intervals, so the animals were fed every five minutes. After the experiment was over, the researchers noticed that the dogs were continuing to salivate at regular intervals. The researchers timed the periods between salivations and found that the episodes occurred precisely five minutes apart, even though no bell had been rung and no food had been provided. Somehow the dogs *knew* when five minutes had passed, although they certainly could not tell time in the conventional sense.

Your Body Knows What Time It Is

Human beings also display an ability to gauge the passage of time to some extent, although the ready availability of mechanical timekeeping devices has probably blunted the efficiency of the human biological clock. The Bowery-el phenomenon described by psychologist Karl Pribram offers convincing evidence that this time-sensing ability exists in humans.

Dr. Pribram found that when the noisy elevated transit line running above New York City's Bowery and Third Avenue was finally torn down, people whose apartments were located along its route "awakened periodically out of a sound sleep to call the police about some strange occurrence they could not properly define." It was discovered that they were awakening at precisely those times when the trains had previously roared past their windows.

Just as the dogs had learned to measure the five-minute intervals between feedings, these sleeping humans had become habituated to the time schedule of the Third Avenue el. The "strange occurrences" they reported to the police were nothing more than the loud silences that had suddenly replaced the once-thundering elevated trains.

Fortunately, most of us are not regularly awakened by el noises; we rely instead upon a mechanical alarm clock to rouse us in the morning. But could you, if necessary, wake yourself at a predetermined hour without the external prompting of an alarm bell? Perhaps you have done this. If not, you might want to try it as an experiment. Research subjects who have attempted to waken themselves at pre-set times have been able to do so with a great deal of accuracy; indeed, many people report that they generally wake up just before the alarm clock rings.

The extent to which human beings have become more dependent on mechanical clocks than on their built-in biological pacemakers is illustrated by a popular practical joke played by college roommates on one another. While the victim of this joke is sound asleep, his roommate turns his alarm clock ahead two hours. If the clock had been set to ring at 8:00 A.M., it rings at 6:00 A.M.

Invariably, the victim will get up, wash, dress, and leave for his day's activities, although he feels that something is wrong, that he hasn't gotten enough sleep. He usually suppresses this message from his biological clock, and it is only when he looks at a clock on his way to class that he realizes what has happened.

Additional evidence for the existence of a human biological pacemaker has been found in experiments with hypnotism. A subject may be given the post-hypnotic suggestion that he will, without consulting his watch, say the word *April* at 20-minute intervals after awakening. And, once awakened, he will indeed perform the required task at approximately 20-minute intervals.

Some scientists object to this sort of evidence for the

biological pacemaker; they think that people can pick up cues from the surrounding environment to assist them in measuring time's passage. For instance, an individual might be able to awaken himself just before the alarm clock rings each morning because at that precise moment his building's ventilation system speeds up and creates vibrations sufficient to wake him. Or traffic might begin to build up outside his window at the same time each day. The post-hypnotic subject, similarly, may receive cues from the activities taking place around him which assist in measuring the passage of time.

These objections sound persuasive and can only be countered by looking at the situation of an individual who is cut off from all external cues. If, in such a situation, he is able to maintain his normal patterns of behavior with respect to time, it would be fair to say that his built-in pacemaker is an accurate biological clock.

Living Beyond Time

Such an experiment was conducted by a French cave explorer, Michel Siffre. Siffre spent 63 days underground in the Scarasson Cavern, a glacial cave 375 feet below the surface of the earth in southeastern France. Since Siffre spent these two months in darkness, cut off from all external time cues, he described his situation as being "beyond time."

During his 63 days and nights in the cavern, Siffre's activities were monitored by sensing devices comparable to those attached to astronauts. They produced a cumulative record of the amount of time he remained awake each day and the amount of time he slept. It soon became apparent that although Siffre was without external means of gauging the passage of time, he very quickly resumed a 24-hour day. He spent roughly two-thirds of each 24-hour period awake and one-third asleep, just as he would have behaved if equipped with a mechanical clock.

True, Siffre's 24-hour day did not follow the clock time on the earth's surface. He might awaken at 5:00 P.M. surface time, remain awake until 11:00 A.M. the "next day," and then sleep again until 5:00 P.M. The important point is that his own biological pacemaker was capable of keeping Siffre to his regular schedule, without the need for external prompting. His body rhythms became a highly accurate clock.

What are these biological rhythms that contribute to the accuracy of our psychological pacemakers?

The body provides several sources of repetitive rhythms for time psychologists to explore. Most obvious, of course, is the heart, whose beat is literally under the control of a biological pacemaker. A healthy heart will beat at a rate of about 72 times per minute; so each set of six heartbeats measures off a period of five seconds. Psychologists who have studied the ability of individuals to estimate the duration of short periods of time have often found it necessary to caution a subject against keeping track of his heartbeat: attention to this built-in clock, or "ticker," is considered a form of cheating.

Other bodily processes follow definite and repetitive rhythms, including respiration, pulse, and the rate at which nutrients are converted to energy. Since these processes are less observable and more subtle than the heartbeat, they have only attracted occasional interest from scientists searching for the biological pacemaker.

Alpha Waves Affect Your Time Sense

One subtle bodily rhythm that has received increasing scientific attention is the electrical activity of the brain, particularly the slow brain waves called "the alpha rhythm." Alpha waves are patterns of electrical activity that occur about ten times a second in your brain when you are relaxed. There appears to be a strong link between alpha waves and the sense of time. Researchers who studied the brain-wave patterns of mystics in trance states report that these individuals produce a high proportion of alpha waves while meditating. Since one important aspect of meditation is a heightened sensitivity to time, the notion developed that the alpha rhythm may be an important biological basis for our sense of time.

A Czech neurophysiologist, Josef Holubar, recently attempted to test this notion. He attached a group of research subjects to brain-wave recording devices, permitted them to relax until a definite alpha rhythm was established, and then tested their ability to estimate short periods of time. He then exposed these subjects to photic stimulation, patterns of flickering light, designed to block the formation of alpha waves. When he retested their ability to estimate time, he found significant differences in accuracy between the alpha and non-alpha phases of the experiment. Holubar concluded that the alpha rhythm of the brain may well be an important biological pacemaker.

Holubar's finding that a change in the alpha rhythm caused a change in his subjects' sense of time was consistent with a great deal of evidence indicating that changes in body rhythms generally do affect the sense of time. This evidence, again, tends to support the existence of a biological pacemaker in the body.

Dr. H. Hoagland was a psychologist who became interested in the effects of changes in body temperature on the sense of time. When his wife fell ill with a fever, Dr. Hoagland instructed her to count up to 60 at the rate of one number per second. He found that her psychological minute passed more rapidly than a minute of clock time. Since an elevated temperature increases the speed of bodily rhythms, it seemed to Dr. Hoagland that his wife's biological pacemaker had accelerated and sped up her sense of time.

If you have ever had a high fever, your own experience was probably similar. When your temperature reached 103 degrees and you felt that it must be time to watch the six o'clock news, the three o'clock soap opera was probably just going on. When your biological pacemaker races, real time seems to drag slowly by.

This process also works in reverse. When body temperature is lowered, bodily rhythms slow down and the biological pacemaker decelerates. After their rescue from a 1906 mining disaster, a group of French miners who had been buried beneath a coal field for a frigid 21 days were asked to estimate the duration of their imprisonment. Responding to biological pacemakers slowed by exposure to the cold, the miners unanimously replied, "Four or five days, at most." And Michel Siffre, the subterranean adventurer I mentioned earlier, reported that during his 63 days underground, his ability to estimate time slowed down by half. When a period of 14 hours went by, it felt to him as though only 7 hours had elapsed.

A similar situation is experienced by the elderly person whose bodily rhythms are slowing down naturally. As his biological pacemaker undergoes a corresponding deceleration, his inner sense of time's passage also winds down in relation to clock time; he experiences that familiar malady of old age, the feeling that time is passing him by.

Ironically, the fact that several types of bodily rhythm are associated with our sense of time has created serious scientific objections to the very notion of a biological pacemaker. Critics of the biological approach complain that there are so many separate body rhythms, each pulsing away at its own unique rate, that it would be impossible for all these rhythms to combine into a single biological clock following one distinct rhythm of its own. Therefore, these critics have turned to the mind in search of the psychological pacemaker.

9

Your Mental Pacemaker

We have seen that scientists who accept the biological-pacemaker theory believe that body rhythms form a kind of sense organ for time, just as the parts of the ear form a sense organ for sounds. This assumes that time is out there, surrounding our bodies, just waiting to be sensed. Partisans of the mental-pacemaker viewpoint look at time from a different angle. They maintain that the mind has the ability somehow to organize your experiences in terms of time.

How might this work? The mental-pacemaker theorists point out that the mind is subjected to a constant barrage of information from the environment, a kaleidoscope of sights and sounds, sensations and perceptions. If this massive stream of stimulation were permitted to enter the mind unchecked, we would soon be flooded with a confusing and disorganized welter of information.

But your mind is more than a passive receiver of messages from the environment. It actively filters and organizes the information flowing in from your senses and determines which aspects of the world around you should be attended to and which should be ignored. Your mind classifies the messages entering from outside in a way that helps you make sense of your experiences.

Think of it this way: Before information enters your mind, it is as confusing and disorganized as a dictionary that lists words in random order. Just as the dictionary's author must alphabetize his thousands of words so that their definitions may be easily located and understood, your mind must "alphabetize" your experiences by organizing them so that they make sense.

Your mind has several tools available to help it organize your experiences, methods for classifying information as it enters from the environment. Your ability to perceive space is one of these tools. Through space perception, your mind classifies objects that you see, whether they are near or far, high or low, left or right. Without space perception, you would be unable to cross the street; you'd have no way of judging how far away any approaching car might be.

Another of the most important tools for shaping and organizing the information that enters your mind is your sense of time. It enables your mind to classify events into such categories as before and after, first and last, sooner and later, brief and lengthy, simultaneous and nonsimultaneous.

The mental-pacemaker researchers have attempted to discover how the mind uses its sense of time as a tool for making sense of its experiences. They have wondered why different events have differing effects on the perception of how slowly or quickly time is passing. Why, for example, do the 15 minutes you spend in a dentist's waiting room seem to pass by in a flash, while the 5 minutes he spends drilling your teeth seem more like 5 hours?

These scientists have also asked whether people with different sorts of personality have different ways of sensing time. Research has uncovered a number of answers to these questions, findings which will enable you to understand how your mind acts as a pacemaker controlling your relationship with the t-factor.

Try the Time Estimation Test

The basic research tool used by mental-pacemaker psychologists is the time-estimation experiment. You can perform this simple experiment right now:

Look at your wristwatch and check the position of its second hand. Now close your eyes and wait until you feel exactly one minute has elapsed. Check your watch again. How many seconds actually went by during your psychological minute?

> Your estimate was ___ seconds under a minute.
> Your estimate was ___ seconds over a minute.

Did you underestimate the minute? Overshoot? Or were you exactly correct? Most people tend to underestimate the duration of a minute by between 5 and 15 seconds. This shortfall occurs because the mind is far too distractible to be able to make accurate estimates of time spans as long as a minute.

Dr. Robert Ornstein, a research psychologist at the Langley-Porter Research Institute in California, has done extensive research into the mind's ability to estimate the duration of time. He has accumulated persuasive evidence that the accuracy of your mental pacemaker depends to a large extent on whatever activities your mind engages in.

Dr. Ornstein documented what you have surely experienced yourself: Time seems to pass much more slowly when your mind is occupied with a complicated task than it does when you are working on something simple. For one experiment, Dr. Ornstein prepared three tape recordings of musical tones, each tape lasting exactly 9 minutes and 20 seconds. The tapes did differ, though, in terms of complexity. The first tape was the simplest; it played 40 tones per minute. The second tape was twice as complicated, playing 80 tones per minute. The third tape, containing 120 tones per minute, was the most complicated of all; listening to it required the most psychological work.

Dr. Ornstein reasoned that the more complicated the tape, the longer it would seem to play, even though there were no real differences in actual playing time between the tapes. He played his tapes for 24 research subjects and asked them to estimate the amount of time that passed as they listened to each one.

Their estimates supported Dr. Ornstein's theory. On average, they felt that the first and simplest tape had run for only 6 minutes and 33 seconds, while the more complex second tape seemed to last 7 minutes and 58 seconds. The third and most complicated tape was estimated to last the longest time of all: 8 minutes and 27 seconds. These subjects' psychological pacemakers seemed to be powerfully affected by the kind of task they were doing. You also probably noticed that these subjects invariably underestimated the time that passed during all three tapes, just as you probably did in your own time-estimation experiment.

One practical implication of Dr. Ornstein's findings may be found in your experiences with boredom. When you are watching a tedious movie or play, time seems to drag slowly by. If someone asked you why you felt bored, you'd probably say, "Watching this movie is hard work." And you'd be exactly right. The more mental work a situation requires of you, the longer it seems to take.

Through a variety of imaginative experiments, Dr. Ornstein was able to verify his discovery that time seems to pass slowly in situations that require a lot of psychological work. He was, for example, able to demonstrate that research subjects who were shown two kinds of geometric figure—simple four-sided forms and complicated many-sided forms—for exactly the same lengths of time felt that they had spent much more time looking at the complex figures. Other subjects felt that more time had passed while they watched a film strip divided into many brief segments than during an undivided film of identical length. In both cases, the more complex a task and the more psychological work it required, the longer it seemed to take.

Try Reading Backward

Why not confirm these findings with a brief and simple experiment of your own? Pick up a book and turn to the last page. Check the second hand on your watch, and then, starting with the final word, begin silently to read the book backward. A book that ends "And they lived happily ever after" would be read "after ever happily lived they and," and so forth.

Stop reading when you feel that exactly one minute has gone by. Then make a note of how many seconds have actually elapsed during your psychological minute.

Now turn to the beginning of the story and read it normally for a period of time you again estimate to be exactly one minute, once more noting how many seconds actually elapsed:

Done? Record the results below:

Backward reading: — seconds actually elapsed.
Forward reading: — seconds actually elapsed.

If you are like most people, your minute of backward reading felt a great deal longer to you than a minute of forward reading. So most likely, many more seconds elapsed before you felt a minute had gone by in the backward reading task than passed when you estimated a minute of forward reading time.

You can appreciate the results or your experiment by realizing that since backward reading is a more complex task than forward reading, your mental pacemaker responds to this increase in work by slowing down; as a result, you feel more time is passing by.

In a way, your experiment and those conducted by Dr. Ornstein suggest that your sense of time is an elastic band, expanding and contracting in response to messages from the outside world. When the messages are complicated, difficult, and require a lot of psychological work, the band expands and more time seems to pass; when the messages are simple and require little psychological work, the band contracts and time seems to go by more quickly. The mental pacemaker, then, seems to be powerfully influenced by the differences in the tasks you perform in the course of the day.

But not everyone's mental pacemaker responds to events identically. Everybody seems to have his elastic band tuned to a different frequency: Some people generally experience time as passing by very quickly while others usually feel that time elapses quite slowly. Some mental pacemaker psychologists have therefore speculated that people of contrasting personality types may be differently attuned to the t-factor.

By looking at what these scientists have discovered, you may be able to understand better how your personality influences the tempo of your own mental pacemaker.

How to Find Your Time Image Score

Dr. Robert Knapp of Wesleyan University has developed a method for determining the tempo of your pacemaker by studying how you visualize the passage of time. Below is a list of 25 images that a writer or artist might use to symbolize time. Place a check next to the 10 images that you feel are most effective in expressing or picturing your own personal experience of time:

_____ 1. A large revolving wheel
_____ 2. A spinning top
_____ 3. A road leading over a hill
_____ 4. Budding leaves
_____ 5. An old man with a staff
_____ 6. A winding spool
_____ 7. A fast-moving shuttle
_____ 8. A bird in flight

———— 9. A speeding train
————10. A quiet, motionless ocean
————11. A burning candle
————12. A stairway leading upward
————13. A tedious song
————14. A spaceship in flight
————15. Wind-driven sand
————16. An old woman spinning
————17. Drifting clouds
————18. Marching feet
————19. A vast expanse of sky
————20. The rock of Gilbraltar
————21. A fleeing thief
————22. A devouring monster
————23. A dashing waterfall
————24. A string of beads
————25. A galloping horseman

Once you have chosen your ten images, give yourself one point for each of the following key images, if you checked it: 2, 6, 7, 8, 9, 14, 18, 21, 23, 25. Add these points together and record the result below:

$$\text{Time-image score} = \text{————}.$$

Your time-image score will range from a minimum of zero (if you checked none of the key images) to a maximum of 10 (if you selected all of the key images). When you examine these ten key images, you will discover that they all depict time as a rapid, dynamic forward motion. The higher your time-image score, the more you tend to experience the t-factor as a swiftly moving force in your life.

High scorers tend to think of time in images that relate to speedy, swift movement. If you earned a score above 5, your psychological pacemaker is set at an accelerated tempo and time seems to pass by quite rapidly for you. If your score was below 5, you experience time as a rather slow and static factor in your life. Your psychological pacemaker is set at a leisurely tempo, and time seems to pass quite slowly for you.

Some of Dr. Knapp's research subjects fell into the first group, picturing time as swiftly moving images; others visualized time as slow moving and static. He therefore wondered whether the personality features of these two groups of individuals differed in other respects as well.

One area in which Dr. Knapp and a colleague, J. T. Garbutt, sought such differences was in the degree of achievement motivation displayed by members of each group. Achievement motivation, a personality feature of great interest to psychologists, relates to an individual's need for success and accomplishment in his life activities: Is he a go-getter or a sit-at-homer?

The standard method for measuring achievement motivation is a psychological test called the Thematic Apperception Test (or TAT for short). The TAT is a collection of pictures depicting people performing various activities, alone and with others. The subject is required to tell a story based on each picture. His stories are examined and scored to assess the prominent themes of his personality. The need for personal achievement is one of the most important themes emerging from many TAT stories.

One TAT picture, for example, shows a young man sitting at a table on which there is a violin. A person with a high degree of achievement motivation might tell the following story:

> This boy is about to practice on his violin. He plays very well, but constantly strives to improve his ability. After much practice, he will realize his ambition to become a great concert violinist and gain fame and fortune as a virtuoso.

You can clearly see how this test response reveals the individual's high level of achievement motivation. When the entire TAT is given and scored, a researcher can obtain an accurate estimate of an individual's level of achievement motivation, whether low or high. Dr. Knapp and Dr. Garbutt did just this with 73 research subjects, obtaining an achievement score from each. They then compared subjects with high achievement motivation to those with low achievement motivation to see if these two groups differed in terms of time imagery.

The findings were striking. Individuals with high achievement motivation tended strongly to picture time in terms of swift forward movement; subjects whose images of time were slow and static tended to fall at the low extreme of the achievement motivation spectrum. So your own score on the imagery test can give you a good notion of the connection between the tempo of your psychological pacemaker and your degree of achievement motivation.

How Motivated Are You?

If your images of time were dynamic, swift, and forward-moving, you are probably an achievement-motivated go-getter; there never seem to be enough hours in the day for you. If your images were still and static, achievement may not be a striking theme in your personality; there always seems to be enough time for everything you do, and sometimes, perhaps, there seems to be too much.

Working with another colleague, Paul Lapuc, Dr. Knapp also studied the connection between time imagery and the personality trait of introversion. Reserved in social situations, more comfortable by himself than with others, an introvert is generally somewhat shy and aloof—in extreme cases, a "wallflower."

Knapp and Lapuc used a psychiatric rating scale to divide 49 research subjects into an introvert group and an extrovert group. They then administered the time-imagery test to all subjects. Introverts differed markedly from extroverts on the imagery test, preferring the static and slow-moving images. Extroverts tended to select the swift, forward-moving images. For introverts, then, time seems to move slowly. If you are introverted to some degree, your psychological pacemaker is tuned to a slow frequency, and you may have the feeling that time is passing you by. If you are extroverted, you barrel through time at a heady pace.

Introverted people tend to be thinkers rather than doers; extroverts seem more action-oriented than thought-oriented. Some researchers have therefore speculated that thought-oriented individuals may feel time is passing slowly for them; action-oriented types may feel that time moves quite rapidly.

Psychologists Charles Buchwald at Downstate Medical Center and Sidney Blatt at Yale University used a psychological test to divide 27 research subjects into a thought-oriented group and an action-oriented group. Each subject was asked to estimate the length of a time interval. When the estimates were compared, Buchwald and Blatt found that time indeed seemed to pass more slowly for thought-oriented subjects.

You might recall my description in Chapter 6 of the thinking type and the sensation type. It is striking that the time-frame orientation of the thinking-type (or thought-oriented) person is extremely broad—encompassing past, present, and future—while the orientation of the sensation-type (or action-oriented) person is quite narrow and confines itself to only the present moment.

Putting these facts together with Buchwald and Blatt's research, it is clear that if you fit into the t-type description, your pacemaker pursues a calm, leisurely tempo, and time seems to move slowly for you. But if you are an s-type, your action-oriented pacemaker pursues a rapid pattern and time seems to pass with great haste. So your psychological pacemaker is influenced by a number of aspects of your personality.

Some psychologists have also attempted to trace the tempo of your pacemaker backward in time, to determine how its speed or slowness developed originally. Drs. Seymour Fisher and Rhoda Lee Fisher of Baylor University in Texas sought to discover whether a connection exists between an individual's early experiences with his parents and the tempo of his psychological pacemaker.

The Fishers believed that strict and ungiving parents tend to dole out attention to their children in small quantities while lenient parents tend to lavish much more time on their children. So they predicted that children of strict parents might tend to overvalue time, just as a poor child tends to overvalue money, regarding a nickel as a large amount of money while a rich child regards it as small change. The children of strict parents may then be expected to develop slow psychological pacemakers in an attempt to stretch small amounts of time. The time-rich children of lenient parents would be expected to become time-spendthrifts, making no attempt to stretch out their experience of time.

To test this imaginative theory, the Fishers administered a psychological test to 54 research subjects. The test consisted of drawings depicting parents and children in a variety of situations. Subjects were required to tell a story explaining each drawing. On the basis of these stories, the subjects were divided into two groups: One group perceived parental figures as strict and dominant; the second group perceived parents as easy-going and lenient.

Each subject was then asked to estimate the duration of a time interval. As predicted, the subjects who perceived parents as strict and domineering tended to overestimate the time interval, to make it seem longer than it really was. The second group did not display this tendency.

The Fishers demonstrated that early life experiences have a powerful impact on the speed or slowness of your psychological pacemaker. If you perceive your parents as having been strict and miserly with their time, it is likely that your psychological pacemaker pursues a slow and leisurely pace. Time seems to pass quite slowly for you because it is a precious commodity and not to be wasted. If your parents disbursed their time freely, your pacemaker was probably calibrated at a speedy rate. You feel that unlimited amounts of the t-factor are available to you and you spend time freely.

10

Your Biomental Pacemaker

In our search for the psychological pacemaker in your body and your mind, we have all but pretended that these are two separate entities. In reality, your body and mind are welded together into one functioning unit. Time psychology therefore has a great deal of unfinished business to attend to. It must discover precisely how your biological pacemaker and your mental pacemaker work in conjunction to determine the quality of your experiences with the t-factor. Hopefully, painstaking research will provide a detailed description of what might ultimately be called your biomental pacemaker.

A beginning has already been made in this direction. On the assumption that your brain is the place where bodily processes and mental processes merge and combine, some researchers have attempted to discover biological brain mechanisms that control your mental experiences of time. How do these biological mechanisms enable your mind to organize information from the environment in terms of time?

The simple experiments you performed have demonstrated that complicated experiences seem to last longer than simple experiences because they require more psychological work. Since psychological work seems to slow the psychological pacemaker, it might be productive to discover how your brain goes about doing such work.

Here is a "poem" written by a neurophysiologist, Warren McCulloch; it's an example of a task requiring a great deal of psychological work:

> Inmudeelsare
> Inclaynoneare
> Inpinetaris
> Inoaknoneis

Were you able to decipher the poem? If not, you will find it simpler to read it in this form:

> In mud eels are
> In clay none are
> In pine tar is
> In oak none is

Why was it so much quicker and simpler to read the poem in its second form? Only because the information in the first version was not organized into familiar word units. The second version was classified into meaningful elements (words), so your mind could readily absorb it.

Psychologists would say that the information in the second version was coded in a way that made sense to you, coded into 11 familiar words rather than into four collections of jumbled letters.

This is why it took you much less time to understand the poem when it was coded in a familiar way. The more familiar your experiences, the less work your mind has to do to code them so they make sense. And, as a result, the more quickly time seems to pass. Doesn't a novel composed of familiar words read more quickly than a difficult textbook of identical length?

How you experience time thus seems to depend on how

difficult or easy it is for your brain to code your experiences into a meaningful form. How does your brain do this coding? Dr. Karl Pribram and his colleagues studied the effects of electrical stimulation on the brain of man's closest biological relative, the monkey. The results suggest that two brain areas —the frontal association cortex and the posterior association cortex—play an important role in the coding process.

When Pribram's team stimulated the posterior (hindmost) portion of a monkey's brain surface, they found that information from the environment was permitted to enter the brain in complex form and was not easly uncoded. When the frontal portion of the brain was stimulated, information was allowed to enter in simplified, well-coded form.

This research suggests that during complex experiences that require a lot of psychological work, the posterior portion of your brain slows down your sense of time. When you read

Inmudeelsare,

your posterior cortex (or brain surface) decelerates your psychological pacemaker, giving you time to decipher this complex, uncoded collection of letters. But when information is already well-coded, as in the sentence

In mud eels are

your frontal cortex takes over and speeds your sense of time.

The frontal cortex, in effect, is your pacemaker's accelerator and your posterior cortex is its braking system. In your travels through time, when you encounter an experience or billboard that is complex and difficult to read, like NOENTRYDEADEND, your posterior cortex slows your mind down so it can absorb the sign's meaning. When the billboard is already coded and simple to read—NO ENTRY, DEAD END— your frontal cortex takes over and speeds up your sense of time.

Your brain, then, seems to be the biomental pacemaker that controls your experiences with the t-factor. It is sensitive to biological rhythms as well as mental processes and is tuned in accordance with your personality patterns. Your brain— part body, part mind—is the engine of your time machine.

Part Three

TIME TRAPS, TIME BOMBS, AND TIME DISTORTIONS

11

The Tyranny of the Past:
Depression and Nostalgia

Each of us maintains powerful but generally unspoken assumptions about the t-factor in our lives. One of the most important of these beliefs is our attitude toward the past. Most often, this attitude reflects the resignation of the old saying: "What's done is done."

Like most examples of conventional wisdom, "What's done is done" (or WDID, for short) is falsely true and truly false. Since it represents an attitude toward time that lies at the core of a serious time trap, it is worthwhile to look closely at WDID through the lens of time psychology.

As I showed earlier, your psychological past is an ever-expanding sector of your time frame. It is constantly receiving an influx of new experiences. Whatever is done in your life enters your psychological past and becomes a part of your me-feeling.

Your psychological past is the attic of your mind, the storeroom to which you consign experiences, thoughts, and feelings. Whatever is done in your life, then, winds up there. But is the past ever really done? Finished? Ended?

No. As we've also seen, the psychological past is constantly called upon to keep you functioning effectively. You are continually required to retrieve items of information from your mental storeroom. To accomplish this retrieval, you naturally use your memory.

So far, this system seems marvelously one-sided. All your experiences, good and bad, are stored in the psychological past. But memory is employed only to retrieve the ones you need, the useful experiences. As to the unpleasant experiences, what's done is done. Right?

Why Memory Is a Two-Edged Sword

Wrong. Memory is a two-edged sword. Without its upper blade cutting through the confusion of daily life, we could not survive. But the under-edge of the memory sword is dangerous: The sharp fact is that your memory is not always under your control. The storeroom of your psychological past is capriciously managed; its door swings open at inconvenient intervals to release unpleasant recollections, too.

To understand how this involuntary treachery of your memory can lead you into a time trap, it is helpful to maintain some perspective on how memory works in general. While people have always believed that memories are stored inside the brain, scientists have only recently begun to pinpoint the precise methods used by the human brain to retain details of the psychological past.

Two distinct and professionally competitive groups of scientists—sometimes called the drys and the wets—have been attacking the problem of memory from different angles. The drys have concentrated on the electrical activity of the brain as it relates to memory. After all, what could be drier than electricity? The wets have focused on the chemical substances manufactured by the brain as the key to the psychological past.

One of the most important of the drys, Canadian psychologist Donald Hebb, persuasively maintained that memories are built of electrical circuits in the bain. According to Dr. Hebb, when you have an experience—let's say you see a sign that says EAT AT JOE'S as you ride to work—a certain group of nerve cells within your brain fire in a random series.

This assembly (or circuit) of nerve cells represents your experience of seeing the sign and is called a memory trace. A new memory trace is similar to a set of footsteps in freshly fallen snow. Once a person has left his first slight trace or path in the snow, people who come by directly after him will tend to follow in the trail he has blazed, making the path deeper and more distinct until it becomes a major thoroughfare or roadway through the snow. But if no one happens to come along soon after the first person, the path will become obscured by drifting snow and will soon disappear.

How Memories Are Built

Like the first set of footsteps in the snow, a new memory trace or circuit of nerve cells will become deeper and more firmly established if it is restimulated soon after it develops in the brain. If you pass the identical sign on your way to work every morning, each time you pass it the circuit of nerve cells containing your memory of the sign will become more permanently established in your brain. The memory trace will become a fullfledged memory. EAT AT JOE'S will be firmly rooted in your mind. But if you never again see the sign, the memory trace will soon disappear like a shallow path in drifting snow. The circuit of nerve cells that held this memory will disconnect.

Dr. Hebb's theory of memory was widely accepted. One of its major repercussions was the squelching of an old wives tale about the psychological past, namely that everything that you experience in life, no matter how transitory or trivial, is retained in your movie camera and tape recorder of a memory and may, under the proper conditions—hypnosis, dreaming, psychoanalysis, LSD—be recalled to life.

This is nonsense. Each of your experiences becomes a memory only if it traces a deep enough track through the nerve cells of your brain. Unimportant events are retained only momentarily and quickly disappear. Which is really a good thing, since neurophysiologist Warren McCulloch estimates that a "man's head would have to be the size of a small elephant" to store each and every memory trace that passes through it.

Dr. Hebb's dry theory of memory was useful but incomplete. How, other scientists wondered, did these circuits of nerve cells develop and maintain their interconnections?

One of the wet researchers, neurochemist Samuel Bogoch of the Foundation for Research on the Nervous System in Boston, believes that chemical bridges are built up between the nerve cells in a memory circuit. These bridges consist of substances called glycoproteins which, essentially, are made up of one or several sugar molecules attached to protein materials.

As a demonstration that glycoprotein bridges are crucial to the establishment of memory circuits, Dr. Bogoch trained a number of pigeons to peck at a target in a certain time sequence. Some pigeons were taught the task very briefly. Others were given much practice so that they remembered the task quite well. Dr. Bogoch then liquefied the brain of each pigeon, submitted it to chemical analysis, and measured the amount of glycoprotein it contained. He discovered that the brains of the pigeons who had a good memory for the task contained much greater concentrations of glycoprotein than the brains of the poor-memory pigeons.

Putting the discoveries of Dr. Hebb and Dr. Bogoch—a dry and a wet—together, scientists interested in how the brain preserves past experiences have tentatively concluded that memories are made up of electrical circuits facilitated by chemical bridges. When an experience is brief or trivial, the chemical bridges do not have time to be built and the memory trace is lost.

Your psychological past, then, contains only those memories that have etched themselves into nerve circuits in your brain. But while your brain is ruthlessly shedding memory traces that don't have what it takes to become memories, it is also fiercely protecting those nerve circuits that did pass the test. In so doing, your brain safeguards the integrity of your psychological past. This, as we'll soon see, is a mixed blessing.

Your brain preserves the memories that make up your psychological past by employing the redundancy principle. Just as a sky diver always takes along an emergency parachute in case his first one fails—a second parachute that is redundant in the sense that it duplicates the function of the first one and probably won't need to be used—your brain relies on more than one nerve circuit to retain a specific memory.

Psychologist Karl Lashley described how this redundancy principle works. Dr. Lashley was interested in the effect that destruction of brain cells would have on memory. He taught a research animal to perform a certain task and then surgically removed a portion of its brain. The animal continued to perform the task. Lashley removed even more of the animal's brain. The animal still remembered what he had to do. No matter where on the brain Lashley destroyed brain cells, as long as the animal had some cells left, his memory remained.

After repeating this experiment many times, Dr. Lashley proposed what he called a mass-action notion of memory. Essentially, this means that memories in your brain are not restricted to one small circuit of nerve cells, but are distributed among a number of nerve circuits massively dispersed throughout your brain.

Therefore, once an experience is admitted into your psychological past by being translated into nerve circuits, it is there to stay. But the biochemistry and electricity of memory are distressingly impartial. Your memory processes work in the same way, regardless of the impact that certain memories may have on you, just as a vacuum cleaner picks up valuable coins and worthless pebbles indiscriminately. And when a memory nerve circuit becomes a negative time force in your life, you may fall victim to your psychological past and be caught in the time trap of depression. Let's examine this trap.

Watch Out for Marley's Chain

In *A Christmas Carol,* Ebenezer Scrooge was visited by the ghost of his former partner and fellow skinflint, Jacob Marley. One of the most frightening visual aspects of Marley's ghost was the fact that he was fettered by a massive length of heavy chain, which he shook "with such a dismal and appalling noise, that Scrooge held on tight to his chair, to save himself from falling into a swoon."

A time psychologist would say that this chain was really Jacob Marley's psychological past. When Scrooge asked why Marley was fettered, the ghost replied, "I wear the chain I forged in life. . . . I made it link by link, and yard by yard; I girded it on of my own free will, and of my own free will I wore it."

Sometimes, your own psychological past may become a Marley's chain; when this occurs, you have fallen into the time trap of depression. Marley had no way of knowing that each link of his chain was really a memory circuit in his brain; but he did realize quite clearly that what was done in the past was not really over and done with at all. Past deeds often link themselves into a chain whose weight, as Marley shows us, is enough to snare the individual who is traveling through the time in his life and to imprison him in the coils of his own psychological past.

What exactly is the time trap of depression? Depression is an affliction so widespread that one psychologist, Dr. Martin Seligman of the University of Pennsylvania, has called it the common cold of psychopathology. But the word *depression* is used so loosely that we must be careful to establish precisely what it means. It is *not* merely sadness, *not* only unhappiness, and *not* simply disappointment. While these three feelings are similar to depression in some respects, there is one crucial difference: Sadness, unhappiness, and disappointment are feelings that life imposes upon you; t-factor depression is a feeling that you impose on yourself.

When Marley says, "I wear the chain I forged in life," he reveals the key element that makes depression a self-imposed time trap: guilt.

And guilt is the belief that your feelings of sadness, unhappiness, and disappointment are your fault. That you deserve them. That they serve you right. Guilt is psychological punishment for past "misdeeds," punishment imposed on you by a one-person prosecutor, judge, and jury: yourself.

So the time trap of depression works this way: t-factor depression is a chain of guilt-laden memories that extends from your psychological past to ensnare you in feelings of unworthiness, helplessness, and passivity.

Think of t-factor depression as a memory chain attached to an anchor. The anchor consists of a "crime" that you committed in the past. The chain is forged of your guilty memories of this alleged misdeed. The anchor–chain combination forms a time trap that pulls your attention and energies away from the concerns of the present moment and away from your plans for the future—an anchor and chain that pull, drag, and haul you relentlessly back into the psychological past.

And the most ironic aspect of the depressive time trap is this: You do it to yourself.

How Depression Slows You Down

How does a person—more importantly, how might *you*—fall into the time trap of depression? To answer this question, we'll need to examine two aspects of this time trap: process and predisposition. The word *process* refers to how your mind stores and retrieves items of memory from your psychological past. The word *predisposition* identifies those features of your personality that may render you particularly vulnerable to the time trap of depression.

By what process can an event in your psychological past become an anchor impeding your progress through time? Some psychologists have called this force the sharpening–leveling process. To understand its impact, it is necessary to add one more bit of information on how your mind stores experiences in your psychological past. We've already seen that memory circuits are so well protected in your brain that they are virtually indestructible. What's done is merely waiting, tucked away in loops of dry electricity that are linked by wet protein bridges.

But memories do not remain constant: Changes and alterations inevitably set in when you recollect an event as it recedes into your distant psychological past. Your brain is not a safe-deposit box where memories remain fixed and unchanging. With the passage of time, they are subtly altered and filtered through the screen of your subsequent experiences and more recent memories.

Now sharpening and leveling become important. Sharpening makes certain of your memories stand out quite clearly from the mass of your stored-up experiences. (When you performed your Landmark Analysis in Chapter 4, your responses consisted of your three most sharpened memories.)

Leveling is the drop-out process of your mind. Through it, many of the complex details of your experience are filtered out of memory, leaving only the sharpest items of recollection behind.

If you have ever played the game of Telephone, you have witnessed an informal demonstration of the sharpening–leveling process. In this game, a group of players forms a circle. The first player whispers a message into the second player's ear, and the message is passed along until it returns to the first player. If the first player began the game by whispering, "The advent of manmade satellites and rockets to the moon opened up a new era in space exploration," the last player might finally whisper back to him: "Adventurers on satellites opened up the moon's exploitation."

You can see that several of the words of the original message were leveled, either by being dropped completely or altered, while the words *satellite* and *moon* were sharpened.

Even if you've never played Telephone, if you have ever returned home from a long trip, you probably discovered how much you had sharpened and leveled your memories during your absence. While you probably retained a clear and sharpened image of some details—the view from the window or the color of the piano—you probably leveled other details, perhaps the wallpaper design in the kitchen or the color of the shower curtain. When you return home, you are able to correct the sharpening and leveling by refreshing your memory.

And this is the catch that makes sharpening and leveling the key processes in the time trap of depression. While you can return to your home from a trip and de-sharpen and de-level your memories of its contents, you generally cannot return to the precincts of your psychological past to correct distorted memories of your previous "misdeeds." Remember: Sharpening and leveling can alter your memory of past events by highlighting some aspects while eliminating others. When the resulting memory is guilt-provoking, it becomes the anchor in your time trap of depression.

The weight of this time-trap anchor can be overwhelming and irresistible. One psychiatrist, Erwin Straus, quotes one of his depressed patients as saying: "I want to get something back to my mind that seems to have gone; to let me see the present or future rather than to keep me looking toward the past."

Self-Punishment Doesn't Fit the Crime

A more detailed history will further illustrate the power of sharpening and leveling processes in the time trap of depression. A 48-year-old man, whom we'll call Charles W., entered psychotherapy after a string of business reverses. His pattern was unchanging: He would build each of his businesses from a struggling and marginal operation into an almost-profitable enterprise. Then he would make a clearly disastrous decision which would wreck the business and return him to square one.

His was a style of behavior often seen in time-trapped individuals: Whenever he seemed to be getting ahead, he found it necessary to punish himself. He acted as though he wasn't good enough to warrant the rewards of success. He seemed to court failure and to crave punishment.

But why? What "crime" was sending chains of memory from his psychological past to enmesh him in failure? After several sessions, his therapist decided to focus on this patient's relationship with his late father, whom he depicted as "a no-nonsense guy, but with a heart of gold." His father had been a civil-service clerical employee and had expected Charles, his oldest son, to carve out a far more lucrative and rewarding career than he himself had attained.

At one point, speaking of his father, the patient broke into tears. He was remembering an incident that occurred when he was 22. He had argued with his father. He could not recall the details of the argument but did remember ending the fight by shouting "Go to hell!" and storming out of the room. Two days later, his father had suffered a heart attack while shoveling snow in front of his house. He never recovered completely and, several months later, he died.

Here was the patient's "crime"—telling his father to go to hell right before his heart attack. He had blamed himself for his father's death and his guilty memories of the argument had been forged into a chain which pulled him back to the past whenever he seemed about to attain happiness.

Had he, asked the therapist, ever discussed the argument with other members of his family who had been present at the time?

No, replied the patient. He'd been too ashamed. He thought that his family had held him responsible for the death

The therapist then made an ingenious suggestion. Would the patient invite one of the family members to their next session to help put the argument with his father into some perspective? Reluctantly, the patient agreed.

"I'll Dance on Your Grave"

The patient was accompanied by his sister to the next session. The therapist asked her to recount what she could recall about the argument. "It was shortly before Daddy died," she began, and the patient sank down in his chair.

"Charles had gotten Daddy mad by suggesting that he was not as strong as he used to be. Daddy was a very proud man—he'd been quite an athlete—and he told Charles to mind his own business. Charles got mad and told Daddy that he ought to get some help in doing chores around the house and said that Daddy was hurting his health by not slowing down."

At this point, the patient straightened up in his chair and watched his sister with an expression of curiosity mingled with confusion.

"Daddy said something like, 'I'll live to dance on your grave,' and Charles really got angry. He said, 'If you won't listen to reason then you can go straight to hell!' And he left the room. And that was the argument."

The therapist turned to his patient, who said, "I hadn't remembered any of that." He asked his sister, "Are you sure that's what happened?" She nodded.

While Charles W. had just learned what really had happened on that day 26 years earlier, it is apparent what had taken place in his mind in the years following his father's death. His memory had sharpened and leveled the argument stored within his psychological past. The sharpening process had highlighted his own anger and his angry "Go to hell!" It leveled away the context of the argument, the feelings of concern for his father that had caused it, leaving as a residue only a nonexistent emotional crime that made him feel guilty over his father's death.

Sharpening and leveling are aspects of a broader mental process: selective memory. Charles W. had selected the guilt-provoking aspects of the argument with his father; he thereby had constructed for himself the chain and anchor of the *depressive time trap.* A different person might have selectively remembered only the concern for his father that had fueled the argument and gone through life with few feelings of guilt draining his energies and handcuffing him firmly to the psychological past.

What impels some people to selectively remember guilt-provoking aspects of the psychological past while others preserve a broader and healthier perspective? This leads us to the second factor in the depressive time trap: predisposition.

Some people seem tuned into the psychological past to a greater degree than others, which leaves them more vulnerable to the selective forces of sharpening and leveling. What are the predisposing factors in this time trap?

Do You Live in the Past?

One of the most powerful factors predisposing a person to the depressive time trap is a time frame that is orientated toward the past. Do you recall the feeling-type individual described in Chapter 6? This sort of person seems to live predominantly under the sway of his or her psychological past; he is perpetually being undone by what has been done in the past.

Quite often—as we saw in the case of Charles W.—the feeling-type distorts the psychological past to provide a seemingly rational explanation for difficulties in the present. The pattern of Charles W.'s life seemed to indicate a need to fail in the present to atone for a crime committed in the past. It was his destiny to fail. And how, he wondered, could he hope to overcome his destiny?

This type of helplessness and passivity in the face of the psychological past is the most powerful factor predisposing an individual to the depressive time trap. Some psychologists, notably Dr. Martin Seligman, have come to regard depression as the result of a "learned helplessness" that becomes the central force in the psychological past. According to Dr. Seligman, most depressives wear an invisible tatoo that says, "I'm a Born Loser."

How might you fall into the depressive time trap? According to the learned-helplessness theory, if your experiences in the past have taught you that your actions make no difference in what you get out of life, you are susceptible to this time trap.

Two types of parent seem most likely to raise depression-prone children. The first type is extremely frustrating. No matter what the child does—whether he behaves well or badly —the parent offers no reward. The psychological past of such a child will eventually adopt the theme of "What's the use?"

When the child grows up, his life will be marked by brooding over the wrongs inflicted upon him by his parents, and he will lack a sense that his actions can produce results. So he drifts into passivity and hopelessness. And, as much as he blames his parents for his woeful state, there remains a pervasive sense that he himself had been unworthy of receiving a response from his parents. If he is a helpless tool of fate, he tells himself, he must somehow be to blame for this condition. So he feels guilty as well as helpless, a combination that adds up to the depressive time trap.

The second type of parent likely to raise depression-prone children is the precise opposite of the first type. This is the sort of parent who denies his child nothing. The parent who spoils his child may not realize just how much spoilage is really taking place. College clinics are bursting with affluent students with no apparent reason to be depressed, but who are, nonetheless, quite depressed. Suicide among well-off young people occurs at an increasing rate. It seems that a psychological past containing memories of an overprivileged youth is just as depression-producing as total deprivation.

Why? If a child is rewarded at random, regardless of whether or not he has earned the reward, he soon learns that what he gets out of life has no relationship to what he puts into it. He learns that he is helplessly dependent upon external forces. His sense of self-worth never really develops. He feels a certain degree of contempt for himself, a contempt which turns into guilt as he inevitably falls short of the expectations he has set for himself. And so he becomes depressed.

How Depression-Prone Are You?

Were your parents nonrewarders? Did they meet most of your actions with a lack of consistent response? Or was your childhood an endless gravy train? In either case, you may be predisposed to the depressive time trap. One simple test to determine your susceptibility to this time trap is to respond to the following—

In order to succeed in life, a person:

‎   ——1. Needs to have a lot of luck
‎   ——2. Needs to work long and hard

If you checked item 1, you probably feel that your own actions are largely irrelevant to what happens to you. Your psychological past may contain a high degree of learned helplessness, and you may therefore be a good candidate for the depressive time trap. If you checked item 2, you feel that you have some degree of control over your fate; while not immune to t-factor depression, your psychological past provides you with strong defenses against it.

Are there ways to avoid the depressive time trap, to escape the anchor-and-chain of the psychological past? There are several self-help techniques for coping with or preventing the tyranny of the past when it unleashes the passivity and helplessness of t-factor depression. (We should note in passing that some forms of depression are caused by physical or biological rather than psychological factors, frequently occurring in the later decades of life. For these biogenic depressions, medical treatment is most effective and should be sought.)

The Single-Jeopardy Technique

As we have seen, memory circuits that contain the psychological past are subject to selective alteration and time distortion. Charles W. was fortunate enough to find a "witness" who could correct the distortions that were poisoning his psychological past—after serving a 26-year sentence! You may not be lucky enough to have a witness. Or perhaps your "crime" was not an overt action but a malicious thought or act of omission.

In these cases, it may be helpful to bring your problem with the t-factor out in the open. Ask yourself: How long a term of guilt do you deserve for your crime? One month, four months, a year? Generally, you'll discover that you've already served your guilt-time twice or three times over. To serve another sentence—or to continue your present sentence—will expose you to emotional double jeopardy. Once you are able to examine your guilt in this open fashion, you may find that the anchor and chain of the depressive time trap have fallen away. After all, even Jacob Marley was looking forward to completing his sentence and relinquishing his chain.

The Time-Projection Technique

Dr. Arnold Lazarus, a behavior modification specialist at Rutgers University, uses the t-factor itself to counteract the depressive time trap. You may find his method helpful in dealing with your own experience.

Dr. Lazarus's technique combats the tyranny of the past with a healthy dose of the future. He suggests that a depressed individual mentally project himself into the future and imagine performing pleasant activities at various intervals forward in time.

One of his patients, a 27-year-old depressed art student, performed the time-projection task while hypnotized (although hypnosis is not necessary for time projection). Dr. Lazarus first suggested that she imagine herself 48 hours into the future, saying, "Enough time has elapsed to have started a painting or done some sculpting. You may even have enjoyed a ride in the country and attended a concert. Think about these activities; picture them in your mind; let them bring a good feeling of pleasant associations, of good times."

Gradually, Dr. Lazarus instructed his patient to project herself further forward in time: a week ahead, then three weeks, then a month, finally six months. At each interval, she was instructed to picture herself, in vivid images, engaged in a rewarding activity. At the conclusion of her entire time-projection sequence, which was completed in just one session, the patient felt that her depression had lifted. Dr. Lazarus reported similar one-session success with other depressed patients.

Why does time projection work? At first glance, it might seem that Dr. Lazarus believes that the passage of time is itself a healing force and that his method is an attempt to speed up this process. Actually, his notion is that time itself has no healing properties; rather, the rewarding and pleasant activities that occur during the passage of time lift feelings of depression. His time-projection technique allows an individual to crowd a host of rewarding and pleasant images into a very brief period of time so that feelings of t-factor depression may quickly be dispelled.

To apply the time-projection technique, three simple rules should be followed:

1. As you mentally project yourself forward in time, choose brief intervals at first and imagine yourself engaged in specific pleasant or rewarding activities; these must be activities that you actually *do* engage in while you are not caught in the depressive time trap.

2. Your images should be as vivid, detailed, and true to life as possible; they should call forth pleasant emotional associations.

3. As quickly as possible, transform your projection into reality by actually engaging in the pleasant activities you imagined.

The Graded-Mastery Technique

If your psychological past has been poisoned by learned helplessness, you can escape from the depressive time trap by cultivating a feeling that your personal actions have an important impact on your fate. In other words, you must unlearn the helplessness of your psychological past.

Dr. Martin Seligman describes a graded-task assignment that has proved effective as an unlearning with severely depressed patients. One depressed patient began with a simple task—making a telephone call. Gradually, as she learned that her actions were having a real effect on events that happened around her (and were provoking responses from others), she progressed to more difficult tasks, unlearning her helplessness as she went. Other patients began by reading a short paragraph out loud and progressed to more challenging tasks until they felt effective enough to engage in debates with other patients.

While your t-factor depressive helplessness is presumably not so severe, your depressive experiences may also be alleviated by the graded-mastery technique. Let's say you're a salesman who has drifted into the passive helplessness of t-factor depression and have been unable to write out an effective sales presentation. You might try to combat your t-factor depression with the graded-mastery technique in this way:

1. Go into the kitchen and make yourself a cup of coffee. A simple task completed.

2. Write a brief letter to a relative. Address it and mail it. This gives you the feeling of having completed another task, however simple.

3. Get in your car and take a ride. Concentrate on how effectively you maneuver and control the vehicle.

These early assignments are designed to provide you with a sense that you can deal with tasks effectively. A feeling that you are not helpless. The graded-mastery technique sends you back temporarily to basics as a way of developing—actually, redeveloping—your feelings of mastery.

By gradually increasing the difficulty of the tasks, you'll soon feel effective enough to write the sales presentation. Or to send back improperly prepared food in a restaurant. Or to demonstrate your sense of mastery in any number of ways.

Once you feel effective and in control of your fate, you will no longer suffer the helplessness, passivity, and self-contempt that form the anchor and chain of the time trap of depression.

Nostalgia: Blasts from the Past

"The past is a foreign country. They do things differently there."

So begins L. P. Hartley's novel of bittersweet recollection, *The Go-Between*. These two sentences, although psychologically somewhat inaccurate, set the tone for our exploration of the second major time trap sprung by the psychological past: nostalgia.

I don't mean the faddish "fun" nostalgia promoted by enterprises turning out imitation Tiffany lamps and ersatz feather boas. The brand of nostalgia we'll be considering is not a fad. It's a time trap. While depression is a time trap that imprisons a person in the guilts and helplessness of the psychological past, nostalgia is a time trap used by a person who wants to return to his psychological past. As such, it can at times represent a deeply troubling emotional process.

To distinguish the time trap of nostalgia from the mild form of interest in the past that leads some of us to pay fifteen dollars a ticket to watch a revival of a 1940s musical comedy, it will be useful to trace some of the history of nostalgia as an emotional disorder.

A Swiss philosopher and historian, Jean Starobinski, discovered that the term *nostalgia* was coined in 1688 by Johannes Hofer, a fellow countryman. At that time, Switzerland was a magnet for exiles from many lands. Hofer observed how these unfortunates would pine and grieve for their native soil. To describe their condition, Hofer combined the Greek words for *return* and *sorrow,* which produced the word *nostalgia,* which in literal translation means return-sorrow, or homesickness.

This term seems to capture the quality of nostalgia more accurately than Hartley's description. To the nostalgic individual, it is not the past that is a foreign country, but the present. Instead, the past is similar to the exile's homeland, a native country full of well-ordered and understandable routines, in contrast to the confusion and foreigness of the present.

As so often happens, after Hofer minted the term *nostalgia,* people began to realize that it aptly described their experiences, and an epidemic of nostalgic illness promptly broke out across Western Europe. By the late eighteenth century, Europeans believed that nostalgia could become fatal and avoided extensive travels away from home.

In the early nineteenth century, a pioneer psychiatrist, Phillipe Pinel, described the symptoms of this spreading disease: "The principal symptoms lie in a sad, melancholy appearance, a bemused look, eyes at times haggard, countenance at times lifeless, a general disgust, an indifference toward everything."

More recently, of course, nostalgia has ceased to be regarded as a major public health menace. Newly fashionable illnesses have displaced nostalgia in the public imagination. Today, sexual dysfunction seems to hold center stage.

In a way, this lack of interest in nostalgia is unfortunate. While nostalgia is not, and probably never was, the widespread psychiatric illness it was once believed to be, it does constitute a time trap that impairs the relationship of many people with the t-factor. As Madame de Stael once remarked, nostalgia can at times become "the most disquieting sorrow that can take possession of the soul."

Since the essence of nostalgia is the powerful desire to live in one's psychological past, an effective method for determining your predisposition to this time trap is to examine the valence (or attraction) exerted upon you by your own psychological past.

Turn back to your Landmark Analysis in Chapter 4. How many of the experiences you listed could be described as pleasant ones, events you might enjoy reexperiencing?

When Was Your Life Best?

How long ago did each of these pleasant experiences take place? When you divide your current age in half, do your pleasurable events occur during the first half of your life (so far), or do they happen in the less distant, more recent psychological past?

Understandably, your susceptibility to the time trap of nostalgia tends to increase as your pleasurable landmarks grow increasingly distant from the psychological present. If you are now 40 years old and had two pleasant landmarks that occurred at ages 26 and 32, you may consider yourself less susceptible to nostalgia than a person of identical age whose pleasant landmarks occurred at ages 6 and 11.

Why? It seems that nostalgia-prone people have some difficulty in mastering the challenges of adulthood and therefore yearn for the seeming simplicity of their earlier years. Dr. Starobinski, in fact, defines nostalgia precisely as "the conflict between the exigencies of integration into the adult world and the temptation to conserve the unique status of the child."

So memory plays as important a role in the time trap of nostalgia as it did in that other tyranny of the psychological past, depression. Again, sharpening and leveling are key processes in your nostalgic experiences. The nostalgic person levels the unpleasant aspects of his psychological past while selectively sharpening his recall of its pleasant occurrences.

While a certain amount of wistful longing for the native homeland of your psychological past is inevitable and natural, do you feel that too many of your thoughts, feelings, and energies are backwardly directed? If this is the case, it will be useful for you to focus on the question of what is missing from your current life that beckons so attractively from your psychological past. Although it is a universal truth that "you can't go home again," you *can* incorporate some of the useful values of your psychological past into your present life.

Many have discovered that one of the most effective methods for dealing with the time trap of nostalgia is the recognition that living in the past is not really living at all, since life is a process of continuous change and development. As the noted science writer, John Pfeiffer, has remarked, "Memory, our recall of the past, exists above all to serve and shape the future."

12

The Tyranny of the Present: Impulsivity, Boredom, and Immobilization

Unlike your constantly expanding psychological past and your perpetually contracting psychological future, the dimensions of your psychological present remain unchanged throughout your life. The immediate now—your sense of *I*-ness—defines the borders of your psychological present and nothing in the universe is briefer or more fleeting than this elusive particle in your time frame.

Yet the psychological present, transitory or even specious as it may seem, often plants dangerous time traps in the path of your time machine. These time traps, the tyranny of the present, represent impairments in your capacity to deal with psychological immediacy. In varying ways and to differing degrees, each of the three time traps sprung by your psychological present—impulsivity, boredom, and immobilization—is rooted in the feelings, thoughts, and actions provoked within you by the t-factor in your life.

The Time Trap of Impulsivity

Margo Y., an attractive and successful 42-year-old boutique owner, received a referral for psychotherapy from an unusual source, a judge in bankruptcy court. Since he considered the roots of Margo's financial ruin to be inextricably intertwined with a certain type of emotional difficulty he had often witnessed in his courtroom, the judge had made therapy a condition for granting her a favorable bankruptcy judgment.

As the history of Margo's "illness" unfolded, it soon became clear that she was a classic victim of a present-day tyranny, the time trap of impulsivity. Although her design business was prospering, Margo was constantly penniless and impelled to borrow heavily in order to meet her basic personal needs like rent, food, and clothing. When she proved unable to pay off her creditors, Margo found herself in bankruptcy court.

Where was all her money going? Into autographs. Margo was an impulsive autograph buyer. The walls of her apartment were a gallery of framed letters, documents, and papers signed by famous figures of the past and present.

During her off-hours, she frequented a number of shops along New York's Madison Avenue, stores that specialized in the sale of valuable signatures. As soon as she received payment for one of her textile designs, Margo's eye would be caught by a signature of Pablo Picasso on an art-show catalog or by a volume of poetry signed by T. S. Eliot. She described her state of mind at these times, saying:

> When I see one of those signatures in a gallery, time seems to stand still for me. There's no yesterday and no tomorrow. All I know is that I have to own it. Now. In fact, the few minutes it takes me to hand over the money and receive the bill of sale are almost intolerable. I have to have that autograph in my hands. I have to own it immediately.

Margo's statement exposes some key elements in the time trap of impulsivity. First, of course, there is the impulse itself. While Margo's impulsive need to possess autographs was somewhat out of the ordinary, the fact that she had such an impulse is quite human. All of us are subjected to impulses every day. But most of us do not become caught in the impulsive time trap. For this to happen, one other element must be present—the need to satisfy the impulse *now*.

The hallmark of the *impulsive time trap* is the inability to allow any delay to come between an impulse and its satisfaction. Devoid of either psychological past or future, the impulsive time trap looks like this:

$$A \qquad\qquad NOW \qquad\qquad Z$$

If you think of life as a voyage across the sea of time from point *A* to point *Z*, it becomes clear that the impulsive is adrift on the raft of his psychological present, isolated in a dense fog which obliterates his past and future from view. For the impulsive, whom we met earlier as the sensation type, time does not flow from *A* to *Z*. There is no past and no future. The only reality is his present impulse, his need for food, sex, warmth, possession of an autograph or work of art.

Since future and past are unreal to the impulsive, he cannot conceive of waiting for an urge to be satisfied. The ideas of patience or delay have meaning only for those who have access to psychological pasts and futures. We can conceive of present desires being satisfied at some point farther along our time frames, at a future time when we can look back to the present (now turned into the past) and feel satisfied that we have finally gotten what we once desired.

You can see that the victim of the impulsive time trap lacks two important tools for dealing with the t-factor in his life: memory and anticipation. Without the reassurance provided by stored-up memories of past needs having been ultimately satisfied, the impulsive perceives each new want as an unbearably intense discomfort with no guaranteed end in sight.

To return to my example: Although Margo had bought dozens of autographs and had had that particular impulse satisfied many times in the past, each time she entered a gallery to make a purchase, she felt that this was really the first time for her. The brief delay between paying for the signature and receiving it became no less intolerable for her, since she was receiving no reassurance from her memory of the past. And without the parallel reassurance provided by the ability to anticipate satisfaction of an impulse at some future time, the impulsive is forced to have his needs satisfied *now*.

How do impulsives get to be that way? How do they fall into this time trap? More importantly if you share some of the problems of the impulsive time style, how did you fall into this time trap?

How Impulsivity Begins

Early experiences in life were important in determining your susceptibility to the impulsive time trap. As infants, each of us was an impulsive. Our needs for food, drink, and warmth clamored for immediate satisfaction. It was only later that we learned a skill that psychologists call delay of gratification, the ability to tolerate some passage of time between feeling an impulse and having it satisfied.

A Stanford University psychologist, Walter Mischel, did extensive research into delay of gratification and his findings illuminate some of the factors that enter into the making of an impulsive.

Dr. Mischel attempted to trace the development of gratification delay through time. Working with a Harvard University psychologist, Ralph Metzner, Dr. Mischel devised an ingenious research plan. He offered a group of 126 school children, ranging in age from 6 to 12, a choice between two rewards for participating in an experiment. The children were allowed to choose between receiving a small candy bar immediately or a much larger candy bar to be delivered after one of five delay periods: one day, five days, one week, two weeks, or four weeks after the end of the experiment.

Dr. Mischel found that children up to the age of about 8 tended very strongly to seize upon the immediate but smaller reward; almost none would wait four weeks for the larger reward. But many children above age 9 had developed the ability to delay gratification; 70 percent were willing to wait for the larger reward. Although, as might be expected, the longer the delay, the fewer children were willing to wait it out.

Drs. Mischel and Metzner concluded that, although the ability to delay gratification does tend to increase with advancing age, many exceptions exist: Almost one-third of the older children were *not* able to delay gratification. These were impulsives in the making, and Dr. Mischel sought to learn how they differed from their nonimpulsive peers.

First, and seemingly most important, he discovered that children who could delay gratification were significantly more intelligent than the immediate-gratification seekers. But this does not mean that if you are an impulsive you're necessarily less intelligent than others. For subsequent research suggested that it is not so much intelligence per se that separates the impulsive from his neighbors as it is his backlog of experiences in gaining or missing gratifications from life. If a person has grown accustomed to not getting what he wants, either now or in the future, he will tend to leap at immediate gratifications.

Since more intelligent people tend to be able to arrange their lives so that they obtain greater gratifications in the long run, they can enjoy the luxury of delay; they've learned that eventually they'll be able to get what they want. But Dr. Mischel found that people who grew up without a father's presence in the home also tended to be impulsive gratification grabbers. And so did people from lower-class backgrounds in comparison to those from middle-class environments.

Therefore, if your early experiences were marked by gratification hunger, if you grew up without a father to provide you with steady sources of gratification or in a relatively deprived environment where tomorrow promised no more than today, you are more susceptible to the impulsive time trap than a person whose early experiences provided a steady stream of gratifications.

The impulsive, it seems, learns to jettison the psychological past and future. In fact, studies at the Devereux Foundation's Institute for Research and Training at Devon, Pennsylvania, demonstrated that impulsive individuals experience a real time-frame shrinkage.

How Time Shrinks

A team of four researchers, directed by Dr. Murray Levine, tested the future-time conception of 47 subjects by asking each a series of 21 questions regarding future events. At what age will you retire? When will a man run a three-and-a-half-minute mile?) Some of these subjects were found to have extensive future time frames; they were able to project themselves into the distant future. Others were quite unable to project themselves into the future. Their time frames were dominated by the psychological present.

The researchers then compared how these two groups of subjects fared on a task involving a choice between giving an immediate but poor answer to a question or delaying response long enough to formulate a better answer. Dr. Levine and his colleagues found that the subjects who were able to delay (or inhibit) their responses to questions were those who had also been able to project themselves into the future. The more impulsive subjects, the ones unable to inhibit their immediate responses, were those who had also been unable to project themselves into the future.

These studies show that a victim of the impulsive time trap has really experienced a tremendous shrinkage of his time frame. The impulsive lives in the psychological present, probably as a result of early life experiences in which gratification delayed became gratification denied.

The consequences of falling into the time trap of impulsivity are harsh, both for the impulsive and those around him. The impulsive is often described by others as a "shark in human clothing," and the comparison is apt. A shark goes through life in a state of perpetual hunger. Never sleeping and never resting, the shark cruises through his span of time constantly eating, constantly seeking gratification—right now. Unlike other animals that are able to store food in hiding places to satisfy anticipated hunger, the shark lives in the external present.

As does the impulsive. Leopold Bellak, a New York psychiatrist, has called attention to the impulsive's sharklike or *anaclitic*—a psychiatric term meaning instant-gratification-seeking—way of dealing with other people. The impulsive will often use another person as a means to an end, for gratification of his needs, sexual, social, or financial. Once his present need is satisfied, the impulsive discards the other person without concern or regret.

The Price of Impulsivity

The endless quest for immediate gratification usually harms the impulsive, not just those around him. He often drifts from job to job when his need for immediate success and wealth is not satisfied. He may even find himself in trouble with the law when he follows his angry, greedy, or sexual impulses without regard for the consequences. (Dr. Mischel found that juvenile delinquents were significantly less able to delay gratification than nondelinquents). And, as in the case of Margo Y., some victims of the impulsive time trap are solitary sufferers, harming no one but themselves.

One of the most widespread forms of the tyranny of the present, in which the impulsive's hunger for immediate gratification hurts primarily himself, is habitual gambling. An estimated 75 percent of the American population indulges in gambling to some degree and more than six million Americans are problem gamblers.

Looking at this social disease through the lens of time psychology, we can see that gambling is almost completely under the sway of the psychological present. The essence of gambling is risk, the excitement of risking money in the hope of gaining an immediate payoff. When you compare the immediacy of a gamble on the roulette wheel with the deliberation with which a businessman invests money in an enterprise that takes months to set up and years to yield a profit, the essential contrast between the present-oriented (s-type) gambler and the past-present-future-oriented (t-type) businessman is obvious.

The gambler is an impulsive whose existence is focused on the immediate agony and excitement of risk. To some extent, all of us are gamblers because most daily activities entail some degree of risk. It is the extent to which our lives are dominated by risk that determines whether we fall into the time trap of impulsivity. A growing branch of psychology is studying risk-taking behavior and can help you tune in on some of the risk-taking elements involved in your relationship with the present t-factor in your life.

One important element in your psychological present that determines your susceptibility to the impulsive time trap is called subjective probability. How good are you at estimating the odds for success or failure in your daily activities?

Dr. John Cohen, a British psychologist, once studied the behavior of 1189 people crossing a busy street in Manchester, England. He was interested in determining how far away an approaching car would have to be before each person felt he could safely cross the street. How strong did the subjective probability of survival have to be before the person stepped away from the safety of the sidewalk?

Dr. Cohen found that most of the people he observed would not step off the curb unless the nearest car was at least five seconds away. But he also found a tremendous variability in this risk-taking behavior. Some people seem to be high-risk types, leaving a margin of only three seconds between themselves and the onrushing vehicle; others refused to budge unless the car was fully nine seconds off in the distance.

How Do You Cross the Street?

Your own street-crossing behavior may provide some clues to your personal level of impulsivity. When you step off the sidewalk, do you leave little or no margin for safety between yourself and approaching vehicles? Do you thrill to the risk of an auto's near miss, much as a matador thrills to the closeness of a charging bull as it sweeps past his cape? Or do you demand an enormous margin of safety before you dare to leave the sidewalk?

If your behavior resembles the former case, you fit the impulsive time style and could be a reckless risk-taker in other areas of your life as well. You may be a daring driver, speeding through narrow spaces with too little tolerance for error. You may be a business plunger, risking large sums of money on deals that have a "good feel." Or you may be a romantic plunger, committing yourself to one mate after another, taking little time for forethought or reflection.

All these examples of the impulsive time style involve gambling, the thrill of immediate risk and decision without delay. Some impulsives seek to rationalize their risky behavior by calling it "decisiveness" rather than gambling. A little logical thought and some objective research will show that this is far from the truth and may, if you are an impulsive, help you see more clearly the time trap that is victimizing you.

Decisiveness is an admirable quality. And, as I'll soon discuss, the complete absence of decisiveness is a symptom of another time trap: immobilization. The impulsive who prides himself on his decisiveness is usually misusing the term, restricting it to the immediate act of making a decision. There is more to decisiveness than that. Those of us who are not trapped in the psychological present realize that the psychological past and the psychological future play crucial roles in decisiveness.

When an impulsive buys a car, for example, his eye will be caught by a shiny, chrome-crusted chariot in a dealer's display window. Before he knows it, he has decided. His hand is signing a sales contract and an installment loan agreement. Joseph Lyons, a psychologist at the University of Kentucky, has neatly summed up the state of mind of the impulsive caught in this time trap:

> For the impulsive a problem is never more than a transparent and disposable container for a presently apprehended goal, precisely like the cellophane wrapper around a piece of candy. It holds the answer to a present tension, but it is itself all in the present; it does not pull one toward a future point.

Why Impulsive Is Not Decisive

For the impulsive, the shiny car was like a piece of candy; his wish to own it was his "present tension." His decision to buy the car, which took no more time than it would take to remove the cellophane from a piece of candy, was not an example of decisiveness. Rather, he threw the problem away, like a discarded candy wrapper. So the time trap of impulsivity is the very opposite of decisiveness: It really represents the *fear* of making decisions. In fact, the most common description of an impulsive's behavior is that "he threw caution to the wind."

A nonimpulsive would handle the present tension of wanting to own a new car without being restricted to his psychological present. He could compare prices, performances, and reliabilities of a number of cars, storing this information in his psychological past. He could anticipate the future consequences of this financial investment, shopping around for the best credit terms and evaluating the impact of the purchase on his psychological future. Equipped with a firm sense of the probable outcomes of his decision, the nonimpulsive can act decisively. The impulsive is a decision-avoider.

Studies confirm that gambling often involves a blurring of judgment and an absence of rational decision-making. One feature of the impulsive's time style has been subjected to particular research attention, his belief that wanting something to happen makes it more likely that it actually will happen. In *The Gambler,* Dostoevsky's protagonist often expressed this very idea; he felt that his luck would be improved by his wish that he be lucky.

If you share this feeling (failing?) to some extent, if you live with your fingers crossed, you have plenty of company. Two research psychologists, Rose Marks and Francis Irwin, discovered in separate studies that an individual's personal needs can powerfully influence his sense of subjective probability.

They prepared a deck of ten cards, marking a certain percentage with a large X. Each research subject was told exactly how many marked cards were in each deck. So each subject knew the odds of picking a marked card at random from the deck. The task for each subject was to predict whether or not the next card he picked would be marked.

If three cards out of ten were marked, for example, the subject knew that he had a 30 percent chance of picking a marked card. He would therefore be expected to predict a marked card 30 times in 100 picks. And this is what happened when the subjects received no reward for correct predictions.

But when the researchers told their subjects that they'd receive a small financial payment each time they correctly predicted a marked card, something remarkable took place. The subjects began predicting many more than 30 marked cards out of 100, even though they knew that the odds of success were still 30 percent. This discovery, now called the Marks-Irwin effect, revealed that if you want something to happen, you'll feel that it is more likely to happen, even if you know quite precisely that the odds are against you.

Another name for the Marks-Irwin effect is, of course, wishful thinking. All of us share it to some extent, but most of us keep it within tight limits. In the impulsive, however, the Marks-Irwin effect runs wildly out of control. Dominated by an impulsive urge that permeates his psychological present, the impulsive wishfully tilts the odds in his favor. Since he wants to own a car right now, he ignores the probability of future financial stress. Since she wants to marry a man right now, perhaps even after just one date, she ignores the probability of emotional disaster. The examples are endless.

How to Escape the Impulsivity Trap

If you are in the grip of the impulsive tyranny of the present, you may naturally wonder how to escape this serious time trap. In general, impulsivity is just about the most difficult time trap to overcome and, in its severe forms, is virtually impossible to conquer without professional assistance. The impulsive lacks internal checks and balances on his behavior, which most people obtain from the psychological past and future.

Often, the impulsive needs external controls imposed upon his behavior. A psychotherapist can work with the impulsive to improve his capacity to delay gratification. The therapist attempts to take control of the impulsive's actions, just as a driving instructor uses a dual-control braking system to keep a student driver out of accidents. Groups of impulsives have banded together to impose controls on each other's behavior. Gambler's Anonymous and Overweight Anonymous are good examples of this approach to the time trap of impulsivity.

The road to recovery from the impulsive time trap begins

only when the impulsive recognizes that he has a problem and then is prompted to seek help in dealing with it. If you have seen your own personality mirrored in these pages on impulsivity, you may now be motivated to take steps to escape from this serious time trap.

Boredom: Everybody Is Susceptible

I have compared the impulsive's psychological present to a raft floating from moment to moment between the *A* and *Z* of his life, cut off from past and future by a dense fog.

Sometimes, however, the raft stops floating and stands still, as though caught on an underwater reef. Cut off from his past and his future, the impulsive now finds himself trapped in an *unchanging* present. He is caught in the time trap of boredom.

From what you now know of the impulsive, boredom obviously is exquisite agony for him because he thrives on change, a never-ending succession of immediate gratifications. He is an insatiable stimulation-seeker. But to a lesser extent, all of us share this hunger for stimulation, and so we are all susceptible to the time trap of boredom.

The most dramatic evidence that stimulation-seeking is a universal human quality was uncovered by psychological research into "stimulus deprivation." What would happen, some psychologists wondered, if a person were almost totally cut off from all sensation and stimulation?

An experiment by Dr. Woodburn Heron, a psychologist at McGill University, was typical of many investigations that sought the answer. Dr. Heron studied 29 men who had volunteered to be research subjects. Each was placed alone in a soundproof room and wore goggles that permitted only diffuse and formless light to enter his eyes. A pair of thick gloves, extending from elbow to fingertip, prevented touch stimulation. The room was filled with white noise, a monotonous, droning, changeless hum that masked all sound.

The results of this stimulus deprivation were devastating. Of the 29 subjects, 25 experienced bizarre visual hallucinations while in the stimulus-deprived condition! One subject began hallucinating after only twenty minutes had passed.

A universal pattern masked the hallucinations. They began, for all subjects, as a change in brightness of the light entering the goggles. Then white dots seemed to appear, followed by geometric forms. Finally, complete and vivid scenes were perceived, full of movement and color—so much movement, at times, that many subjects reported feeling nauseous.

Clearly, most of the subjects lost contact with reality after a relatively brief period of stimulus deprivation. They showed symptoms usually associated with severe psychotic reactions. Indeed, in simple mental tests given shortly after the experiment ended, the subjects seemed quite impaired when compared to control groups.

This research, which has been repeated many times with similar results, highlights the central importance of receiving a steady flow of stimulation from the environment. Without this steady flow, we all would soon become psychotic. It is not surprising, then, that all human beings share a common hunger for stimulation. (So do man's animal relatives: A chimpanzee performs difficult tasks when rewarded with nothing more than an opportunity to look through a peep-hole, thereby increasing his visual stimulation.)

How Much Stimulation Do You Need?

It is the degree of your stimulation hunger that determines your susceptibility to the time trap of boredom. Some people are tuned to high levels of stimulation. If you fit this description, you will feel somewhat deprived in situations where a person who is tuned to lesser stimulation hunger would feel quite satisfied. In other words, it will take more stimulation to keep you from becoming bored.

The differences in stimulation hunger between one person

and another became important during World War II when the military had an urgent need for reliable radar operators. The operator's job was to watch a screen for hours at a time and to report the presence of blips, electronic echoes bouncing back from airplanes, when they appeared on the screen.

During training, some men did quite well at this task, but others performed poorly and failed to detect blips. These men reported that they'd found it difficult to keep their minds on the task. They had become bored.

Clearly, some types of people were—and are—more susceptible to the time trap of boredom than others. In order to study and measure differences in such susceptibility, psychologists developed a task called Continuous Perceptual Tracking or CPT for short.

A CPT setup involves a screen and a button. The subject is required to press the button each time a dot of light flashes across the screen. When these dots of light appear frequently, most people do well at the task. But when many seconds elapse between each dot of light, strong differences appear between people's performances.

People with a high level of stimulation hunger, for example, do poorly on a CPT task as the intervals of time between dots of light increase. When an impulsive performs the CPT task, he obtains a low score. The empty intervals of boredom between stimulations are intolerable for him. His mind wanders. His attention is beguiled by extraneous distractions. The more impulsive he is and the more he hungers for immediate gratification, the worse he performs on the CPT task.

How to Test Your CPT

How high is your own threshold of boredom? You can make a quick estimate by performing your own CPT task.

As you read the next five pages of this book, keep a mental count of the number of times the letter *g* appears. Read as quickly as you normally do and do not reread any of the sentences to check your accuracy.

When you reach the bottom of the fifth page, write your mental g-count in the margin. Then go back and carefully underline each *g* that appears. By counting the number of underlinings, you will obtain an accurate g-count. Divide your mental g-count by your accurate g-count. The percentage score reflects your toleration for boredom.

Taking an arbitrary but reasonable figure, if your accuracy is 90 percent or better, you have a relatively high threshold for boredom. Your level of stimulation hunger was, therefore, not high enough to impair your efficiency in performing the task. But as your percentage score decreases, so does your boredom threshold. If you are only 30 percent accurate, your hunger for stimulation is so high and demanding that your attention wandered from the task. As your percentage score goes down, your susceptibility to the time trap of boredom goes up.

This does not mean that a low boredom threshold is inevitably a serious personality defect. Some situations are so inherently tedious that the *absence* of boredom is a sign of psychopathology. When frontal lobotomies were routinely performed on the brains of violently psychotic individuals, many were thereafter content to perform tasks of incredible repetitiousness, such as making a precise count of the number of cornflakes in a carton.

It is when your susceptibility to boredom enters into direct conflict with your style of living that this time trap becomes dangerous. To take an extreme case, imagine an accountant who has an impulsive time style, a rampant hunger for stimulation, and a minimal boredom threshold. Would you want him preparing your tax return? At the other extreme, picture a fireman who has a minimal appetite for stimulation and an extremely high threshold for boredom. He might be well able to tolerate the tedious waiting periods between fires, but when called into immediate action, he would be likely to break down under stress.

These extreme instances may help you draw a frame around the issue of stimulation hunger vs. boredom toleration in your own life. It may be that you—among countless others—have until now been unaware of this aspect of the t-factor in your personal planning. The offices of counseling psychologists and vocational rehabilitation specialists are magnets for dissatisfied individuals who selected their styles of living without regard to the potential tyranny of the psychological present.

Such dissatisfactions are usually the product of t-factor incongruence, the extent to which your daily activities create discomfort in your psychological present. If you want to develop an idea of how much t-factor incongruence exists in your life, you should make two determinations:

1. Where do you belong on the stimulation-hunger vs. boredom-toleration continuum?

Generally, the more precisely you match the impulsive time style and the sensation-type personality and the more poorly you performed on the CPT task, the closer you are to the stimulation-hunger end of the scale. Conversely, if you responded to the description of the impulsive with more shock than recognition and also excelled on the CPT task, you belong at the opposite pole of the scale.

2. How much stimulation, immediate gratification, and excitement do your daily activities provide?

While this must be a highly subjective estimate, subjectivity is an asset here. Two lawyers in the same firm might be poles apart in their estimates of immediate gratification provided by their work. One, a contract specialist, is content to spend hours reading tedious fine print; the other may spend his time engaged in exciting courtroom battles.

By comparing your level of stimulation hunger in 1 to the degree of stimulation provided by your activities as shown by 2, you can obtain a clear sense of how well your time style in the psychological present meshes with your lifestyle. This analysis can pinpoint the sources of vague but persistent dissatisfactions in your psychological present. More important, you may use this t-factor incongruence technique as a tool in guiding your decisions for future changes in lifestyle. If you are able to bring your daily activities into closer congruence with your ways of dealing with the present t-factor, you will be better able to steer clear of the time trap of boredom.

Immobility: Clinging to the Present

There is a type of person who actively seeks the changelessness of boredom, courts the status quo and would prefer to freeze his time machine in its tracks.

He is the immobilized. He seems to be a willing victim of the tyranny of the present. His psychological mannerisms are designed to prevent the present from becoming the past and to ward off the future as it attempts to supplant the present.

While the impulsive craves change for the sake of change, the immobilized seeks changelessness for the sake of changelessness. To the immobilized, the psychological present represents safety and security. He is much like the nostalgic, who yearns for the simplicity and well-orderedness of long ago; the immobilized clings just as tightly to the present moment and feels unable to relinquish it voluntarily.

The most extreme examples of immobilization are the severely psychotic. A chronic schizophrenic patient was observed standing at a corner in New York City, waiting for the traffic light to turn green. When the light changed, he stepped from the curb, stopped, stepped backwards onto the curb again, stopped, stepped down again, stopped, and stepped back up again. By this time, the light had turned red, so he was able to stand still once more, waiting, spared the necessity of changing his position, totally immobilized in his psychological present.

This patient was displaying ambivalence magnified to extremely pathological proportions. His desire to cross the street was precisely counterweighed by his wish to remain on the sidewalk. So, like the horse in "Turkey in the Straw" who "wouldn't go ahead and wouldn't stand still," the patient simply "went up and down like an old saw mill."

Psychotic individuals differ from the balance of the population by the severity of their symptoms and their relative inability to conceal these symptoms from others. The schizophrenic of the street corner did not merely feel ambivalent; he acted out his ambivalence in the poignant spectacle of mounting and dismounting the sidewalk.

In less severe and more private forms, many of us find ourselves immobilized by ambivalence. Sometimes the immobilized time style is so subtle and habitual that it operates beneath the level of awareness, quietly detracting from the quality of life. You might experience a small shock of recognition as you join in exploring this aspect of the tyranny of the present.

If ambivalence lies at the core of the *immobilized time trap,* what precisely is it? With tongue in cheek, one psychologist noted that ambivalence is "the feeling you get while watching your mother-in-law drive over a cliff in your new Cadillac."

Ambivalence is a mental tug of war between two competing sets of feelings which pull you in opposite directions. If the strength of each feeling is in exact balance with its opposite, the tension on your emotional rope can become quite unbearable. This situation is the reverse of the impulsive time trap. The impulsive tolerates no delay in making a decision; the immobilized, hamstrung by ambivalence, cannot make a move in any direction.

One quality shared by many immobilized is obsessionality, the endless hashing and rehashing of all possible outcomes of any action. A person who tends to be obsessional may draw up extensive lists of pros and cons in an attempt to make a decision.

The Case of the Imperfect Bride

A young man contemplating marriage but trapped by his tendency to immobility, listed the desirable characteristics of an intended mate in one column and her undesirable traits in a parallel column. He discovered, to his dismay, that the lists balanced out evenly. Every pro was associated with a con. He decided to delay his decision until he noticed some additional attribute of the young woman that would tip the balance in or out of her favor.

None ever did. Each time he felt that he was on the verge of a decision, his ever-active mind discerned some countervailing consideration that reestablished the balance between his hopes and his fears. His girlfriend eventually became impatient, left him—and took the decision out of his hands.

Avoidance of decision is the essence of the immobilized time trap. Like those citizens of Manchester, observed by Dr. Cohen, who refused to cross the street until no cars were on the horizon, the immobilized is holding out for a sure thing. He is allergic to risk and uncertainty. He clings to the security of his psychological present as though it is a ledge and feels that any movement from it would plunge him into an abyss.

To the immobilized, life seems a perpetual reenactment of Frank Stockton's short story, "The Lady or the Tiger" in which the protagonist is confronted with two closed doors. Behind one stands a beautiful woman. Behind the other snarls a ferocious tiger. Which door will he choose?

The immobilized chooses not to choose. He allows choices to be made for him. He actively seeks out situations where the pros exactly balance the cons. If the immobilized time style is your pattern of behavior, if you constantly choose not to choose, you may well wonder what purpose immobilization serves in your life. Why do you cling to the comfort of the psychological present?

Probably to avoid the consequences of making a decision. When he was asked why he decided not to marry his girlfriend, the young man in the above example replied, "She decided, not me! Go ask her why she didn't want to get married." Sooner or later, or so the immobilized person rationalizes, someone else will make a decision and take the responsibility for its consequences out of his hands.

Almost needless to say, the immobilized pays a penalty for the privilege of indecision. He lives under a great deal of tension. The effects of such tension were dramatically highlighted in a classic study by the Russian psychologist Ivan Pavlov.

Pavlov was interested in learning how a research animal would respond to experimentally-created immobilization. He trained a dog to expect food whenever a round circle of light was flashed upon a screen. Each time the dog saw this circular shape, he salivated in anticipation of being fed. And he was fed, but only when the flash of light was perfectly circular. When the light flash was shaped like an ellipse, no food was delivered, and he soon learned to salivate only when he saw the circle.

Then Pavlov played a dirty trick on the dog—and transformed him into a canine immobilized. Slowly and deliberately, Pavlov tinkered with the shape of the ellipse, making it ever more circular. At first, when the ellipse still maintained an approximately ovoid shape, the dog remained unperturbed. He was still able to distinguish between the circle and the ellipse and determine when he would and would not be fed.

As the ellipse relentlessly melted into circularity, Pavlov's dog seemed torn by a classic ambivalent time trap: It expected both to be fed and not to be fed—simultaneously. As the distinction between the two previously clear-cut choices became hopelessly blurred, the dog fell victim to the tyranny of the present.

The dog had become an immobilized. Pavlov described its behavior: "It began to squeal in its stand, kept wriggling about . . . and, on being taken into the experimental room, the dog now barked violently."

Since people are generally more inhibited than dogs, they refrain from publicly squealing, wriggling, and barking when caught in the immobilized time trap. But privately, the immobilized pays a heavy price for his immobility, including headaches, digestive upsets, and skin rashes.

How to Escape the Immobility Trap

If you share some of the immobilized's self-punishment behavior—ambivalence, obsessionality, conflict between equal choices—what can you do about it?

First, you need to evaluate what purpose or purposes immobilization is serving in your life right now. Are you somehow benefitting from immobility?

A man was unsuccessfully treated by a succession of psychotherapists in an attempt to help him escape from his long-term inability to make a decision, however trivial. Each therapist felt that this patient was thwarting and undermining his treatment, clinging to his identity as an immobilized as though paralysis were an old friend. Finally, he entered therapy once more, made rapid strides, and in a matter of months was noticeably more decisive.

The final therapist possessed no magic whatsoever; in fact, his technique was almost irrelevant. What made the outcome of this therapy different was the fact that the patient's wife had died just before he entered treatment. She had been the decision-maker in the family, and her death made his time style as an immobilized no longer rewarding to him. There was no longer a wife to lift the burden of decision-making from his shoulders. His circumstances, not his therapy, forced him to move.

This case demonstrates a fundamental fact about the treatment of emotional problems: Change will occur only as a result of discomfort. If you are reasonably comfortable with your time style as an immobilized, and if others around you are willing and able to help you remain in this well-cushioned time trap, then your prospects for change are minimal.

But what if your immobility has been a source of stress for you, perhaps a hidden problem, vague and poorly defined? Now that you've labeled this problem, what can you do about it?

Very often, the diagnosis of a problem is a major factor in

its treatment. By identifying your pattern of behavior as immobilization, you may be able to see clearly the forces and counterforces, the emotional tugs of war, that combined to keep you rooted in the psychological present. But unlike the situation confronting Pavlov's dog, your own set of emotional pros and cons is probably not as well balanced as it seems at first. There is usually a factor that will tilt you in one decisive direction. Your task is to bring yourself to search for that factor.

A newspaper editor in therapy, torn between his love for wife and children and his affair with a brilliant female writer on his staff, was unable to make a decision either way, causing both wife and lover great pain. His desire to keep both wife *and* lover had immobilized him in a painful situation. His task was not merely to choose. He had to choose to make a choice and realize that he had to sacrifice something to salvage the situation.

Once this realization sank home, the editor, reconciled that he could not keep all that he had once had, decided that he valued wife and children more than his lover. Others would have made the opposite choice. The important point of this example is that the escape route from the time trap of immobilization is paved with a form of personal sacrifice.

The situation usually faced by the immobilized was summed up by the social psychologist Kurt Lewin as an approach–approach conflict, a conflict between two desirable goals: wife or lover; security in a routine job or potential success in a new career; being taken care of or feeling independent.

In order to break out of this time trap, the immobilized must determine which of his two approach goals is slightly less desirable and then to sacrifice it in favor of the alternative goal.

Making such a choice, while difficult, is not as painful as most people believe. The hard part is to decide that a choice must really be made. Only when he reaches this basic decision does the immobilized become able to mobilize himself into escaping the tyranny of his psychological present.

13

The Tyranny of the Future: Anxiety and Fantasy

The time traps we have explored until now were rooted in reality. No one can doubt that his psychological past and his psychological present are real. Your storehouse of memories and influx of immediate sensations and perceptions can be sorted, classified, arranged, and described. They exist. They are facts. They either are or have been. And like most common-sensical, no-nonsense, modern-day individuals, you probably felt quite comfortable sifting through the facts of your psychological past and present.

In this chapter we will venture into territory that is unreal, the stuff of anticipation rather than memory, imagination rather than perception: the future sector of your time frame.

In particular, we will deal with a pair of time traps, anxiety and fantasy, that are related to your psychological future. Both represent impairments of your capacity to deal with the psychological potentialities in your life. And although these time traps seem to be rooted in unreality, you will discover that the impact exerted on you by this tyranny of the future is only too real.

Something Terrible Is Going to Happen

Ever since the first primitive men and women realized that there is a tomorrow that follows today, people have been asking themselves and each other the compelling question: What is going to happen?

What does the future hold? Is it good, bad, indifferent? Mankind's fascination with the future has been intense throughout history. Soothsayers and astrologers, visionaries and mystics, have lived in high style through the centuries by satisfying their contemporaries' passion for prediction. Today, this hunger is fed by futurists ranging from meteorologists through economists to science-fiction writers and crystal-ball gazers, all profiting from society's seemingly bottomless need to know what is going to happen.

Curiosity about the future is a healthy human trait. It demonstrates an awareness that our present actions and activities will have more than merely immediate consequences. (The impulsive, we have seen, seems to lack this sort of awareness, while the depressive seems not to care about it very much.)

Interest in the future also alerts us to possible threats and dangers. We order coal in summer to be protected from winter's chill. In fact, man's capacity to anticipate the future —an ability believed linked to his highly-developed central nervous system—is one of the prime sources of his superiority over the balance of the animal kingdom.

But anticipation is merely a tool at your disposal. Like most tools, it can be a tyrant as well as a servant. When your capacity to anticipate the future comes to be a negative t-factor force in your life, you are a victim of the time trap of anxiety.

The anxious has an extremely fearful relationship with his psychological future. Instead of wondering, "What is going to happen?" as others do, the anxious thinks to himself, "Something terrible is going to happen." The future sector of the anxious's time frame is like a minefield. The question is not whether or not he will step on a mine. His only question is when?

When what? The anxious is often unable to specify exactly what it is that the future is threatening him with. And it is this vague quality of the anxious's anxieties that give the time trap of anxiety its distinctive stamp.

Psychologists draw a sharp demarcation between anxiety and fear. Fear is your emotional reaction to a specific dangerous situation. When you are afraid, you know what you fear. A soldier pinned down by enemy machine-gun fire is afraid of being killed by a bullet. He feels fear. He knows what he's afraid of. But a postman who is unable to do his job because of a vague but powerful sense of threat and danger does not feel fear. He feels anxiety, the feeling that something bad is going to happen; but what it is, he cannot say.

The Manifest Anxiety Scale

If you are an anxious, you know well that it is this non-specific aspect of anxiety that makes it such an uncomfortable time trap. Dr. Janet A. Taylor, a research psychologist interested in anxiety and its effects on human behavior, developed a brief true–false psychological test called the Manifest Anxiety Scale. A glance at some of its items, answered as an anxious would answer them, will illustrate how all-pervasive a time trap anxiety can be:

1. I am often sick to my stomach: True
2. It makes me nervous to have to wait: True
3. I have very few headaches: False
4. I worry quite a bit over future troubles: True

Items 2 and 4 show quite clearly that a person's psychological future is a prime focus for his feelings of anxiety. His vague feelings of danger and threat are the core of his anxieties. Items 1 and 3 reveal the tremendous impact that anxious feelings can exert on one's physical health. Worrying about unreal events—events that have not yet occurred and may never occur—can have a sharply damaging real effect on your current physical, as well as emotional, well-being.

Dr. Joost A. M. Meerloo, a psychiatrist who has been deeply aware of the t-factor's importance in day-to-day living, describes a form of neurotic behavior which he terms the preparation neurosis.

The preparation neurotic is so concerned with protecting himself from the possible onslaughts of the future that he almost totally neglects the concerns of the present. Sometimes, notes Dr. Meerloo, entire societies may be caught up in a mass preparation neurosis. The fallout-shelter epidemic of the early 1960s is a prime example. People mortgaged their homes and plunged themselves into debt to finance construction of supposedly bombproof havens in their backyards. Many stocked their shelters with food, water, and weapons to repel unfortunates who were less future-oriented than themselves.

Your own life may provide some other examples of preparation neurosis. One therapy patient, a man in his late forties, reported that he had been emotionally preparing himself for his parents' death from the age of 17. He continually found himself rehearsing his feelings and actions upon hearing the bad news, attending the funeral, and, as he put it, "picking up the pieces afterward."

His preparation neurosis made him miserable for 30 years. While the eventual demise of his parents was an absolute certainty—in contrast to the uncertain threat of nuclear warfare—this patient's style of living in his psychological future had clearly deprived him of much happiness and enjoyment in the present.

The What-If Syndrome

Another form the preparation neurosis might assume in your relationship to the t-factor is the what-if syndrome. The guest who arrives for a weekend in the country bringing enormous suitcases filled with clothing to meet any and all atmospheric contingencies, a medicine chest full of remedies for ailments ranging from snakebit to rickets, a library of magazines, books, and games to ward off rainy day boredom, and an arsenal of athletic equipment to protect himself against sunny day boredom, suffers from the what-if syndrome. His psychological future is so fraught with anxieties over possibilities, reasonable and remote, that he is buried beneath the defenses he erects to cope with uncertainty.

Do you find yourself paralyzed by what-if? If so, your psychological future has snared you in the *anxious time trap.* Like the immobilization time trap set by the psychological present, the what-if syndrome can stop you in your tracks. But what-if often provides you with a camouflage that enables you to fool yourself into believing that your inaction is a form of action.

This camouflage is created by a teaming up of the what-if syndrome with the preparation neurosis. A good example of such camouflage is a writer who had some initial success and is now expected to improve upon his previous efforts.

Suddenly, a host of what-ifs pop into the writer's mind. What if I run out of ink? What if my supply of paper runs low? What if the part of town I'm describing doesn't look that way any more? What if someone else is writing a book on the same subject? What if I get writer's block?

In response to these what-ifs, the writer busies himself in a frenzy of preparation. He goes out to buy paper, ballpoint pen refills, and pencils. He spends days in research for background details of his story. He meets with other writers who are also in the throes of preparation neuroses, to assure himself that they're not duplicating his subject matter. He reads books on writer's block and how to prevent it.

He is a very busy man. Not immobilized at all. But he is getting nowhere. In defending himself against the what-ifs lurking in the psychological future, the writer's preparations distract him from the concerns of the present.

It might be well to examine your own collection of what-ifs to discover how much you have mortgaged your definite present to your indefinite, but definitely anxiety-provoking, future. How much insurance do you carry, for example? Some people have been known to pour a huge percentage of their current assets into life insurance, far in excess of their families' realistic needs.

And how much groundwork are you laying down for plans that never materialize? Some people are perpetually about to return to school and earn a degree they've always wanted or to learn a trade that will help them get ahead. But there seem always to be one or two nagging what-ifs to be defended against:

"What if the roof springs a leak and my money is tied up in tuition payments? I'd better get the roof fixed now and go back to school next term. Or what if the work is too hard for me? I ought to borrow someone's textbooks and spend a few months getting back into the swing of studying. But what if I don't have a good place to study? First, I'll soundproof the living room, and then I'll borrow the books, and then . . ."

Groundwork. Preparation. Insurance. These are all effective strategies for defusing the anxieties that may permeate your psychological future. Effective but unproductive, since these methods for coping with the what-if syndrome, at most, shield you from the unpleasant fact that you are caught in a time trap.

Try the Blow-Up Method

Dr. Arnold Lazarus of Rutgers University developed a more useful technique for handling the what-if syndrome. It's called the blow-up method. When you use it to deal with the what-if syndrome, it might also be called the so-what method. It attempts to help patients overcome their what-if anxieties by enabling them to confront and gain some perspective over their presently nonspecific worries.

Dr. Lazarus instructs his patients to carry their anxieties to their farthest extremes, to blow them up from imaginary molehills to imaginary mountains.

One patient was a young man who enjoyed going to the theater. But during intermissions, he would smoke a cigarette in the men's room and, immediately upon returning to his seat, would begin to worry over whether he'd fully extinguished his cigarette butt. What if he had started a fire? he thought in panic. He spent the rest of his time shuttling from his seat to the men's room and back, endlessly checking and rechecking for flames.

To combat this anxiety, Dr. Lazarus gave the patient blow-up instructions. He told him to imagine that a fire had indeed started in the men's room, spread throughout the theater, rampaged out of control through the neighborhood until the entire city was in flames. Soon, many cities are burning in a fiery chain reaction, then entire continents, then the whole world. Finally, the entire universe is blazing away.

The patient followed these instructions. At first, he felt a surge of anxiety, but soon was able to relax and feel some amusement over his anxieties. It seemed that blowing his initial fear way out of proportion enabled him to obtain a fresh perspective on it.

If you suffer what-if symptoms, you might want to try this method for handling your anxieties through exaggeration. Chances are that you will come to regard your former anxieties with some degree of detached amusement and begin to counter your troublesome what-ifs with trouble-resolving so-whats.

The what-if time style is fueled by uncertainty regarding the future. The what-ifer seems determined to perform the impossible feat of stacking the deck in his favor even though, as he realizes quite well, the deck is not in his hands. But the uncertainty of the what-if time style is a source of hope as well as anxiety. Something bad may happen, but perhaps one can prevent it if he tries hard enough. When this trying is brought down to a reasonable level so that it no longer interferes with the tasks of daily living, the what-if individual has escaped from his time trap.

The Fate Neurosis

Some forms of the tyranny of the future, however, lack even the smallest glimmer of hope-giving uncertainty. Rather than fearing that something terrible *may* happen, some anxious individuals are convinced that something terrible *will* happen. These people are suffering from a fate neurosis.

Like the depressives described by Dr. Seligman, fate neurotics seem to go through life wearing a tatoo that says "Born to Lose." The fate neurosis is really a mirror image of depression. While the depressive perpetually hashes and re-hashes the injuries inflicted upon him in his psychological past, the anxious who suffers from a fate neurosis agonizes and reagonizes over the anticipated injuries that he imagines are lurking unavoidably in the psychological future.

Feelings of anxiety in anticipation of some inevitable but vague future misfortune range from a generally mild sense of foreboding to genuinely hopeless, shoulder-sagging despair. Many people recognize the milder manifestations of the fate neurosis in themselves, feelings that may have originated in experiences that taught them to view the psychological future with anxious resignation.

For example, people whose early years were marked by repeated failure and deprivation expect more of the same in later life. Many who were scarred by the great depression of the 1930s, no matter how much their financial situations have improved since then, continue to regard the future with anxiety and dismiss optimism as a form of blindness. Former and present victims of racial or religious discrimination may also find it difficult to imagine that the future will be any better than the past; so they attempt to expunge both of these dimensions from their time frames through alcoholism or drug abuse.

Paradoxically, many people whom life has treated quite well also suffer from symptoms of fate neurosis. One therapy patient, a successful executive in excellent health who was happily married with three affectionate children, reported unshakable feelings of anxiety that "something awful is going to happen to me. One of my kids will be hit by a car, or I'll go blind, or . . . something." He entered treatment after worrying himself into an ulcer, and the roots of his fate neurosis quickly became evident.

He believed that life was almost entirely a matter of luck, and that the law of averages dictated that each good event in life is bound to be balanced by a bad event. "After all," he said at one point, "there's a built-in balance. You're born, and that's the best thing. But you die, and that's the worst thing. It all averages out." His main source of future-directed anxiety was that he'd built up a frightening surplus of good things in his life up to that point. When, he wondered, would time's pendulum swing back at him, redressing the balance?

How to Turn Pleasure Into Pain

This variety of the fate neurosis often takes a slightly different form that might be called there's a cloud in every silver lining. Victims of this time trap share the feeling that a balance exists between pleasure and pain. So, to avoid paying for their present pleasure with future pain, they attempt to fool fate by transforming their pleasurable experiences into painful ones.

Example: A man's daughter comes home with a report

card showing two *A*s and four *B*s. He feels a momentary surge of pride, but says, as gently as possible, "Only two *A*s out of six marks? Oh well, I guess that's all I should expect."

Example: A woman receives a compliment on her new car and immediately says, "It uses too much gas, you know, and we can't really afford the payments. And someone already stole the hubcaps." The implication of this time style is clear: If you feel happy today, you'll pay for it tomorrow. Therefore, don't feel happy today, or else bad luck will catch up to you.

The common feature in these forms of the anxious time trap is the belief that life is a matter of luck. A psychologist at the University of Connecticut, Julian B. Rotter, devoted several years to studying how people differ in the extent to which they feel that they are in control of their destinies in life. Using a test composed of pairs of items such as I feel that success is mostly a matter of hard work *or* I feel that success is mostly a matter of luck, Dr. Rotter instructed test subjects to choose the one statement in each pair that they agreed with.

One item of each pair expressed what Dr. Rotter terms an internal locus of control, that is, a feeling that the individual's destiny is in his own control. The second item expressed an external locus of control, a sense that the individual feels he is more a tool than a captain of his fate.

By giving this test to many subjects, Dr. Rotter became able to classify people according to their locus of control. Internals, he discovered, differ from externals in many respects. For example they display more achievement-motivation, ambition, and leadership qualities.

Are You an Internal or an External?

Most likely, then, your susceptibility to the fate neurosis may be connected to your own locus of control. People with an external locus of control tend to believe their destinies are almost irrelevant to their actions; they are mostly matters of luck and chance. It is easy to see how such a person can persuade himself that his past good fortune leaves him wide open to future woe.

People whose locus of control is internal feel less threatened by the future. If they have become successful, they trace their success to their own efforts rather than to luck; they see no reason to doubt that the future will be filled with more hard-earned success.

It is also easy to see how the external can use his fate neurosis as an elegant cop-out. Since his bleak future is really beyond his control, how can the anxious be held responsible for his misfortunes? Fate is, after all, fate. Some fate neurotics seem almost to crave the disasters that lurk in the psychological future; theirs is an I-told-you-so time style.

Some people, for instance, are so anxious over the prospect of unemployment that their work suffers to such an extent that eventually they are indeed fired. Then they can exclaim, with accuracy, "I told you so!"

This self-fulfilling prophecy, a particular trademark of the anxious, is consistent with the typical story of a businessman who is so worried over something going wrong that he neatly fulfilled his prophecy by developing ulcers.

The self-fulfilling prophecies of the anxious seem motivated by a compelling desire to overcome the uncertainties of the psychological future. The suspense of wondering when that terrible something will happen is intolerable, and the anxious would like to get the dreaded event over with as quickly as possible. This understandable desire occasionally gives rise to what mental health professionals call counterphobic behavior. A person acts counterphobically when he plunges himself directly into a situation that is extremely frightening for him.

An individual who anxiously feels that he is fated to die an early, violent death may act counterphobically by driving his car at high speeds on wet roads or by picking arguments in bars. He seems to be tempting fate—and this is exactly what the counterphobic is up to. He wishes to short-circuit the time between now and the highly-feared psychological future, so he lives dangerously and often fulfills his own prophecy of disaster.

Some therapists have begun to make use of counterphobic techniques in an attempt to free their patients of severe future-oriented anxiety. The blow-up method, which I described earlier, is one example of how counterphobic thoughts can be used in therapy.

Implosive Therapy

A much more extreme behavior modification procedure, implosive therapy, has also been employed with some success. The idea behind it is that many anxieties are unrealistic.

A person may avoid going to parties because of a vague but powerful feeling of anxiety. Since this anxiety keeps him isolated from other people, he is unable to learn from experience that his fears are unfounded—and anxiety perpetuates itself indefinitely.

An implosive therapist's goal is to expose his patient to the anxiety-provoking situation in order to allow him to see that the anxieties contained in his psychological future are unfounded. The therapist may insist that his patient attend a party; he might even offer to escort his patient to the party himself. Once in the situation, the patient's anxieties are likely to melt away in the face of the benign realities. By bombarding the patient with what he fears most, the implosive therapist teaches him that he is able to confront and overcome the anxieties contained in his psychological future.

So counterphobic behavior is an aspect of the anxious time trap and also under proper conditions, a method for escaping the time trap. The choice is between getting the feared event over with and getting over your fear of the event, between fulfilling a negative prophecy and checking to see whether it was an accurate prophecy in the first place.

Awareness of the distinction between tempting fate and questioning whether fate is a negative t-factor in your life is the first step toward overcoming the anxious time trap. As your sense of control over your own psychological future increases, your anxieties will undergo a corresponding decline.

How Fantasy Becomes a Time Trap

One of the most potent time traps arises from the obvious and unavoidable fact that the future is unreal. Since the future does not yet exist, it teems with possibility. While the anxious recoils from the future for fear of what it holds, some people display the opposite tendency and seek to escape into the vagueness and flux of times to come. These are the fantasizers.

Fantasy is a universal experience. All of us are capable of turning away from the outside world of hard-edged reality and tuning into a world of our own creation, where things can be arranged pretty much as we please. Dr. Jerome L. Singer, a psychologist at Yale whose research into daydreaming has been extensive, noted that people constantly alternate between two channels of experience. The outer channel provides awareness of what is happening around us; the inner channel represents the fantasies, daydreams, and unrealistic thoughts that continually stream through our minds.

Fantasy, then, occurs when we turn away temporarily from the real world and attend instead to our inner channels of experience. Through careful research, Dr. Singer and his associates have shown that people tend to daydream more when engaged in monotonous tasks, which in effect turn off the external channel and allow the internal channel to open up. When real-life experiences are varied, changing, or in some way threatening, the external channel is wide open and daydreaming is greatly curtailed.

If fantasy is a normal form of human behavior, capable of significantly enriching day-to-day experiences, when does it become a time trap?

Answer: When fantasy comes to dominate a person's future-oriented thinking to a point where he finds himself tuning out the external channel more and more in preference for his unreal world within.

The fantasizer prefers spinning pleasant reveries about his future life to building a foundation for his future in the present. Perhaps you greatly enjoy discussions of days to come. In conversations you anticipate with relish achievements and attainments that lie ahead for you. If this is the case, you may wish to examine how much of your current energies are dissipated in such fantasy, to what extent you have altered the optimal balance between the outer and inner channels of your experience.

All of us have known dreamers whose entire existence seems mortgaged to the glories of tomorrow. A dreamer might be a mediocre college student dreaming of becoming a nuclear physicist or a great mathematician. Or a post office clerk dreaming of his future as an industrial tycoon. To the extent that fantasy turns these individuals away from taking realistic steps toward achieving realistic goals in life, they are victims of the fantasy time trap.

The common features in most victims of the *fantasy time trap* is a longing to escape into the future, almost a reverse nostalgia. We might call fantasy the Mr. Micawber time trap, after Dickens' fictional character who went through life batting all adversities into the future with the phrase, "Something will turn up." To the fantasizer, the psychological future is an endlessly attractive beacon, uprooting him from the present and detaching him from the painful necessity of living life one day at a time.

"Tomorrow," insists the fantasizer, "will be brighter," but he is usually unable to tell you how this brightness will be ignited.

Something for Nothing

The fantasizer is seeking a shortcut into the future. He abandons the realistic, step-by-step outlook on time that is adopted by those around him. He favors an intuitive approach. Very often the intuitive type, whom I discussed earlier, is likely to be a prime victim of the fantasy time trap. Why not? Intuition, after all, is the psychological equivalent of something for nothing. When you know something intuitively, it has not been necessary to pay for your knowledge by expending effort to obtain it.

If you intuitively know that you will dislike a potential blind date, you are spared the necessity of going through with the date and acquiring your knowledge at some cost.

The fantasizer, too, wants something for nothing. He wants to achieve his life's goals without really striving for them. So he settles for the fantasy of achieving these goals and thereby virtually insures that he'll never attain them. This puts teeth into the time trap of fantasy for fantasy siphons away current strivings in favor of the nonproductive pleasures of the inner channel.

In the words of Percival Symonds, a noted researcher into the psychology of fantasy: "What the person dreams of being, he need not be; what he is, he need not dream of being."

The fantasizer substitutes his dreams of what he wishes to be for any attempts actually to fulfill these wishes. Like Scarlett O'Hara in *Gone With the Wind,* he meets today's unpleasant realities with the hollow benediction, "Tomorrow is another day."

How can a fantasizer escape his time trap? To answer this question, we need to know what keeps the fantasizer fantasizing in the first place? Is he mentally unstable? Are fantasies just a breed of delusion?

Actually, the fantasizer usually does not suffer from a psychiatric disorder. Professionals who work with severely ill psychotic patients have, in fact, often made the surprising discovery that schizophrenics tend to fantasize less than other people; they seem to lead extremely barren fantasy lives.

How Fantasies Grow

Fantasy is a normal part of living. It is believed to arise early in life when a hungry infant does not receive food immediately. As a shortcut, the child attains temporary relief from his hunger by imagining that he is being fed. This is the original fantasy.

Later in life, you can obtain relief from other blocked impulses by engaging in fantasy. Haven't you sometimes found yourself working out angry feelings toward someone in your life by staging an aggressive daydream in which you triumph over your target? This is a common experience and an indication of the valuable role—as an escape valve—that fantasy can play.

Within limits. The infant quickly learns that an imaginary bottle or breast cannot slake his thirst. And most of us need to express angry feelings directly as well as in fantasy. But the fantasizer exceeds these limits, and so it is important to wonder what keeps him going at his fantasies.

One very common factor that contributes to the fantasizer's time style is collaboration from those around him. Usually motivated by kindness, the fantasizer's family and friends often support his leap into the future. Perhaps they become enmeshed in his rosy projections. The fantasizer is often a charismatic person, capable of firing up those around him with enthusiasm. And who wants to be a wet blanket?

Nothing is quite so painful as confronting a fantasizer with the reality that he is dreaming rather than doing. Few relish such a task. It is comparable to withholding drink from an alcoholic or bursting a child's balloon. Separating a fantasizer from his dreams seems tantamount to leaving him with nothing to hold onto. It isn't surprising that the fantasizer's loved ones often seek to shield him from the external channel of reality.

But the choice is not really one between living a life of fantasy and living a life devoid of future-oriented hope. A middle-course is available to the fantasizer, if he and those around him are willing to pursue it. This course was suggested by the work of an early psychoanalyst, Alfred Adler. Dr. Adler viewed life as a struggle to overcome the initial feelings of weakness and inferiority that most of us experience as children.

Each of us, according to Adler, develops an image of what we would like to become later in life, a goal toward which we strive. He termed this goal a "guiding fiction," a fantasied embodiment of our plans and hopes. While it is unrealistic to expect to live perfectly up to a guiding fiction, this fiction is useful as a focus for our actions and efforts.

Unfortunately, the fantasizer's guiding fiction becomes more fictional than guiding. On some level, he realizes this, but clings to the fiction nonetheless, possibly in the belief that there is nothing to substitute in its place. He has painted himself into a psychological corner.

The fantasizer's escape route from the fantasy time trap is a new, more attainable guiding fiction to provide him with a focus for his energies, thoughts, and actions in the present. It will also relieve him of the despair he's really been feeling all along but hiding from himself—and inducing others to help him hide from—by escaping into fantasy.

It may be helpful for you at this point to attempt to spell out in words your own guiding fiction, the ideal self that you wish to become.

Is your guiding fiction attainable, even approximately? What are the steps that must be taken to carry you from where you are right now, in the present sector of your time frame, to the guiding fiction that beckons from your psychological future?

If the steps are too many or too unattainable, you may have saddled yourself earlier in life with an unworkable guiding fiction. Perhaps this caused you to fall into the fantasy time trap.

By reworking your guiding fiction in the light of what you now know to be the facts of your current life and future potential, you will be better able to avoid or escape the time trap of fantasy.

14

Time Bombs

The time traps explored in Chapters 11 through 13 share one important feature: They represent *possible* difficulties in your relationship to the t-factor in your life. And while it is possible that you have been, are, or will be caught in one of the time traps associated with your psychological past, present, or future, it is also possible for you to avoid these time traps completely. They are not inevitable.

But a number of extremely significant problems with the t-factor tend to be universal in our society and occur at predictable intervals during each individual's journey along the highway of time. These problems with the t-factor are potentially disruptive and explosive. They are time bombs planted at strategic locations on your time frame.

Just as the notion of landmarks, borrowed from the field of pediatrics, proved useful in analyzing your psychological past, another concept, borrowed from developmental psychology, will help us understand the placement and potency of time bombs along your time frame: the concept of critical periods.

For many years, research psychologists have believed that an organism's behavior is more powerfully affected at certain times by the surrounding environment than at other times.

Dr. J. P. Scott of the University of Maine, for example, discovered that puppies were most socially responsive to human beings between three weeks and seven weeks of age. During this critical period, the puppies were more amenable to being trained than at any other time. Human beings also go through critical periods in their process of biological development.

The adult human brain is quite specialized, with one-half—generally the left hemisphere—in control of the ability to speak. But if the left side of the brain is damaged during early childhood, an individual will still be able to speak if his right hemisphere takes over the speech function. But should the left hemisphere be damaged in adulthood, the right hemisphere is much less likely to acquire speech capacity. There seems to be a critical period for speech flexibility in the human. After the critical period passes, the speech mechanism becomes relatively locked into place and cannot be transferred to the opposite side of the brain.

Critical periods are built into the life spans of all men and women, points along the time frame at which we are particularly sensitive to, and can be powerfully influenced by, the people and events and challenges that surround us.

So a psychologically critical period becomes a crisis that life imposes. How a person responds to this crisis has an enormous bearing on the quality of his life following the critical period. This chapter will explore four of the post-childhood critical periods that occur in the lives of modern men and women—four time bombs embedded in the path of your time machine.

The crises that these time bombs impose upon you may be managed in a number of ways. They have awesome negative potential, packing explosive emotional forces that can cause real psychological distress. But if you manage them in a positive way, each crisis may represent a step toward emotional health and psychological development.

Time Bomb I: Adolescence

Adolescence is a two-way crisis. With equal justice, you can call it either the end of childhood or the beginning of adulthood. When the time bomb of adolescence explodes—and anyone who has lived through these stormily eruptive and disruptive years of life realizes that *explodes* is the most accurate word—the shock waves rumble with equal force toward the individual from his psychological past and psychological future.

Most of us now realize that childhood, the adolescent's psychological past, is not an idyllic vacation from life's problems as it was once wistfully idealized. Some psychiatrists even regard infancy as life's first built-in time bomb. Otto Rank, a psychoanalyst, elaborated a comprehensive theory of personality around the notion that the birth trauma, the sudden bombardment of the infant with the sights and sounds of the world outside the womb, is a key ingredient in emotional development. Melanie Klein, an influential British psychiatrist, argued that during the first months of life the individual experiences a set of intense emotional crises that determine the later personality.

While these are controversial notions, there is no doubt that childhood experiences establish some important patterns of personality and habits of living. These habits and patterns provide much of the fuel for the time bomb of adolescence.

At birth and shortly thereafter, the human infant is one of nature's most totally dependent creatures. The infant's survival and well-being hinge completely on the care and feeding from parental figures. The early years of life are marked by the child's progression from this total dependence and self-centeredness to an increasing ability to act independently and to interact with others. But throughout childhood, the individual remains largely dependent upon his or her parents for security and survival and therefore feels relatively little sense of power or control over the important details of daily living.

So the adolescent's psychological past is generally dominated by the theme of dependency vs. independence. The experiences that fill out the adolescent's psychological past center on his or her attempts to overcome the condition of total dependence that is the human being's major birthright. But what of the adolescent's psychological future?

To an adolescent, the psychological future is uncharted territory, pocked with a multitude of question marks. What kind of adult will I become? How will I earn a living? Will I be a success? What does being successful really mean? Who will be the important people in my life? Can I make it on my own? Will I always be so fat? So thin? So ugly? So awkward? So incompetent?

An Explorer Without a Map

The theme of the adolescent's psychological future is that amalgam of hope tempered by fear that is best expressed by the word *uncertainty*. The adolescent confronts his psychological future like an explorer planning to enter a wilderness equipped with only the vaguest of maps and the most unreliable of compasses.

Some societies have attempted to alleviate the uncertainties of adolescence by charting specific pathways for the transition from childhood to adulthood. Tribal rites of passage, painful ordeals and the completion of traditional tasks, were effective in defusing the time bomb of adolescence in some cultures. So were structured systems of apprenticeship.

Our modern society offers no such assistance to the adolescent. The rites of passage we offer—graduation ceremonies, wedding ceremonies, the right to vote—seem irrelevant to the uncertainties of adolescence; they occur almost as a matter of course. The adolescent has a vague notion that adulthood has something to do with graduation from school, marriage, and voting; but he also realizes that achievement of these goals will not transform him from a child to an adult. Which is why the psychological future of the adolescent is replete with uncertainties, questions that seem unanswerable.

The adolescent is caught between two forces: his psychological past, with its theme of dependency, which he wishes to escape; and his psychological future, with its theme of uncertainty, which he fears to enter. When these opposing forces are ignited by the profound biological and sexual changes associated with puberty, the adolescent time bomb explodes. How an adolescent handles the crisis created by this critical period greatly affects the course of his adult life.

Dr. Paul H. Seton, a psychoanalyst who has directed the student counseling service at Smith College, feels that the adolescent's relationship to the t-factor during the later teenage years reflects in large measure the powerful conflicts set off by the clash between psychological past and psychological future.

Dr. Seton notes that "developing time perspective is important in many aspects of one's evolution and individuation." Part of the normal crisis of adolescence, in Dr. Seton's view, is a phase of timelessness, during which the teen-ager rebels against the t-factor in his life. The psychological past and the psychological future are ignored, seemingly in an attempt to avoid the dependency of the past and the anxiety associated with the future.

Freed from these fetters, the adolescent feels capable of indulging in behaviors and activities that, in later life, would be considered symptoms of the impulsive time trap. He lives in the present and for the present and often seems to be rootless and aimless. It is customary to call this an identity crisis, but actually the volatile and explosive adolescent is in a t-factor crisis. While he seems to have "taken leave of his senses," he really has taken a temporary vacation from the psychological past and future.

How does the adolescent emerge from this critical period?

Dr. Seton believes that the adolescent finally achieves a "psychotemporal adaptation" by coming to terms with his own remembered past and with his own anticipated future. Rather than running away from his past, the adolescent comes to feel rooted in that past, to use his past experiences as raw materials for future development. Rather than fearing his future, the adolescent develops a number of goals toward which he will strive. "Insofar as one can convey some sense of himself as having been, now being, and where one hopes to be," according to Dr. Seton, the critical period of adolescence has been successfully weathered.

Time Bomb II: Early Adulthood

From the end of adolescence to the beginning of middle adulthood, people enter into a search for stability. As adolescence ends, a person has fixed—sometimes desperately—on an estimate of personal strengths and weaknesses (provided by the psychological past) and a set of personal objectives or goals that seem worth pursuing (provided by the psychological future). The task of early adulthood is the slow but steady attempt to transform potentialities into actualities.

The early adult is expected to trade the explosive uncertainties of teen-age life for an orderly, reasonable, and desirable system of values, and instead of asking troublesome questions, the early adult soothes himself with comforting answers.

The search for stability takes several forms, provided by an obliging society's traditional values. According to Sigmund Freud, psychological health equals the capacity to work coupled with the capacity to love. Traditionally, the early adult seeks to solve both terms of this equation. He finds a job and finds a mate and settles down to let the t-factor do its work of carrying him to the future.

And then the time bomb of early adulthood explodes.

The explosion comes about as a result of the early adult's self-deception, the common belief that passing the age of 21 automatically brings about maturity and adulthood. In reality, the early adult has achieved more the appearance than the substance of maturity. Many early adult males and females are boys and girls in grownup clothing. Their education has not prepared them for a life of work. They have not successfully declared their independence from their parents. They force themselves—and society forces them—to pretend that they have mastered both of these critical transformations.

A child runs away from home and is brought back by a society that tells him: "You're not ready to live independently." But an early adult receives—and believes—the message that he *is* ready to live independently when, in fact, he may not be. So early adulthood has become the as-if stage of life. Young men and women assume adult roles as if they were prepared for them. Often, the result is a form of role-playing.

Therapists who work with patients in their twenties are frequently struck by the fact that these young people are still troubled by the issues of independence vs. dependency that are so powerful in childhood. One patient, a man of 25, complains that he is unable to make decisions and must constantly ask his father for advice. Another patient, a 28-year-old woman, feels stifled by her overbearing husband, whom she married at age 17. But she feels incapable of surviving a divorce and living on her own.

Both patients, and thousands like them, are struggling with the crisis of early adulthood, the belief that maturity is conferred, like a diploma, upon graduation from adolescence. The time bomb is detonated by the discrepancy between the individual's lingering state of dependence on his parents and his belief that he should be completely independent from them.

The fallout from this time bomb often takes two forms: bitter work dissatisfaction, increasingly seen in the 20 to 30 age bracket; and a staggering divorce rate, particularly in the first year of marriage. As a result, psychotherapy, marriage counseling, and vocational guidance have become booming growth industries with an early-adulthood orientation.

If early adulthood is often a charade in which individuals adopt the outward trappings of maturity in order to obtain a sense of independence and stability, another player is often added, a child.

Still struggling with their attempts to achieve independence from parents, the early-adult man and woman now become parents themselves. In many cases, they view the birth of a child as tangible proof that maturity has been achieved. After all, the logic unfolds, it takes an adult to produce a child. Unfortunately, the birth of a child frequently produces the most serious crisis of early-adult life.

The burdensome responsibilities of parenthood may quickly disrupt the artificial stability of early adulthood. Shortly after giving birth, most women experience an emotional letdown, the baby blues—transient feelings of depression that are produced by the physiological aftereffects of pregnancy. Additionally, there may be intense psychological reactions to motherhood: feelings of having been saddled too soon with awesome responsibilities for which the woman is unprepared; resentment over the time-consuming necessities of baby care; jealousy over losing the center of attention; nostalgia for the freedom of the past.

The Dangers of Fatherhood

While the psychological pitfalls of motherhood have long been noted and understood, awareness is growing only lately that parenthood is a crisis and critical period for the father as well. Dr. William H. Wainwright of New York Medical College has presented persuasive evidence that the birth of a child may have a previously unsuspected explosive impact on the child's father. In a paper titled "Fatherhood as a Precipitant of Mental Illness," published in the *American Journal of Psychiatry,* Dr. Wainwright presents ten case histories of men in their twenties and thirties who experienced serious emotional reactions to fatherhood.

What makes fatherhood so potent a time bomb in such cases? Dr. Wainwright notes a number of possibilities. Significantly, most relate strongly to the child's arrival as an event that stirs up powerful conflicts over dependency, conflicts supposedly already resolved and tucked away in the psychological past.

The father may fear that he will be unable to provide adequately for the child; he cannot tolerate the child's total dependence upon him. Or he may become jealous of the child for absorbing too much of his wife's attention; he no longer receives enough mothering from her. He may feel helplessly trapped in the marriage now, the child being a kind of hostage his wife may use to keep him at home. This reawakens dormant feelings of helplessness and imprisonment that he experienced as an adolescent trying to achieve independence from his own parents.

While the men in Dr. Wainwright's case histories reacted to fatherhood with severe emotional disturbance, he made the important observation that "factors precipitating these 'postpartum' reactions in men are not in themselves specific to the mentally ill." On the contrary, fatherhood is one of the built-in crises in the lives of early-adult males, as is motherhood for early-adult females. Rather than providing the hoped-for magical transformation into maturity, a newly-arrived child is too often the spark that ignites a major time bomb explosion in the early-adult critical period.

What can be done to defuse the time bomb of early adulthood? A realistic meshing of expectations with abilities is the most productive way. It is unrealistic to expect an early adult, still declaring independence from his or her parents, to establish and maintain a lifetime marital commitment. It is unfair to insist that an early adult with minimal work experience make an irrevocable choice of occupation. Yet early adults who don't make such choices risk society's label of "immaturity."

Perhaps it is necessary for our culture to admit—rather than deny and conceal—that many (if not most) early adults have not matured totally, to realign what we expect from an early adult, and to bring our aims closer to reality.

There is some evidence of progress in this direction. More early adults allow themselves the necessary luxury of social and vocational experimentation. Trial marriages, job-hopping, postponement of child-rearing, or decisions against parenthood are on the increase.

Society's response to these trends has generally been dismay. Parents ask: "Why don't they grow up and settle down?" Hopefully, society will learn that the answer is: "Because they're just not ready. Give them time."

Time Bomb III: Middle Adulthood

The time between ages 35 and 60 probably makes up your most crisis-ridden years. If a lifetime is a test, childhood and adolescence represent preparation and study periods; early adulthood represents the taking of the test; and middle adulthood is comparable to receiving and evaluating one's marks.

The middle adult finds himself immersed in what had previously been his psychological future. His anticipations, hopes, values, expectations, and ideals had always been aimed at the sector of his time frame that he now occupies.

The early adult asks, "Can I do what I want to do?" The middle adult wonders, "Am I doing what I set out to do?"

If the answer is no, it is easy to understand how middle adulthood may become a period of explosive crisis. But, surprisingly, even if the answer is yes, even if a person has achieved or exceeded his goals, his success may unleash explosive and disruptive t-factor forces.

By middle adulthood, the individual has attained in reality

the stability and maturity that he merely role-played during early adulthood.

He has become a man; she has become a woman. But ghosts from the psychological past linger on, remnants locked in the closet of memory that may ignite through spontaneous combustion. Most often, the scene of this explosion is the marriage relationship.

With statistics showing a spurt in divorces after 20 years of marriage, it is reasonable to wonder how the time bomb of middle adulthood attacks a marriage. A couple who married in their early twenties grew into maturity together. By the age of 45, both have changed and developed in a multiplicity of directions.

Each partner in the relationship naturally wants to have his or her development validated, to receive recognition of the fact that he or she is now much different. And yet the t-factor plays a trick on both spouses. A wife looks at her successful, graying-at-the-temples, insurance-executive husband and sees the awkward 20-year-old college junior she married. A husband looks at his dignified, college-professor wife and sees the chubby, cheerful, sorority president he married.

Each is viewed by the other not only the way he or she *is* but also as he or she *was*. The psychological past is inescapable.

While the backlog of shared experience is crucial to a healthy marriage, by middle adulthood, each spouse also feels a powerful urge to be appreciated for which he has become, unhampered by reminders of what he has been. This urge is often satisfied by an extramarital liaison, a search for an outsider's maturity-validation that a spouse cannot provide.

A 52-year-old married patient explained his need to see women other than his wife:

> If I'm in a restaurant with my wife and I send back a bottle of wine or argue with the waiter, she says, 'I'm proud of you. I remember when you were afraid to do that.' She gives me a pat on the head. But when I'm in a

restaurant with another woman, she has no idea that I was ever afraid to stand up for my rights. She sees me as the tough, aggressive guy that I've become. She doesn't make me feel self-conscious.

This case shows that the middle adult is oddly similar to the adolescent: Both seek to establish independence from the psychological past.

The adolescent complains to his parents, "You're treating me like a child." The middle adult bemoans his mate's inability to separate his present maturity from its roots in the past. Fred McMorrow, a newspaperman and author, has coined the expression *midolescence* to capture the explosive similarities between these seemingly quite different critical periods.

Another term for midolescence or the time bomb of middle adulthood has been suggested by an industrial consultant, Harry Levinson. He calls this critical period "the middle-age crisis."

Levinson has been particularly interested in the emotional impact of middle adulthood on an individual's work life. He notes that during middle adulthood, an individual comes to the traumatic realization that the psychological past has begun to exceed the psychological future. His time frame seems suddenly to have taken a downward tilt. Phrases like "over the hill" and "past my prime" take on a chillingly personal relevance. This shift in the way one views one's time frame often becomes a genuine middle-age crisis. It usually emerges as feelings of sadness, sometimes intensified to the point of despair, and by physical symptoms, commonly fatigue, digestive disorders, and chest pains.

The Seven Parts of Middle-Age Crisis

In his book *Executive Stress,* Levinson identifies seven factors that strongly contribute to the severity of middle-age crisis in our success-oriented society. These factors may be reflected in your own lifestyle during middle adulthood.

1. *Contraction of the hard-work period.* The average age for attaining success in life seems to be diminishing. We feel that less and less time is available to attain our goals. The pressure for quick success (and anxiety over its absence) is one source of the middle-age crisis.

2. *Inseparability of life and career patterns.* We tend to divide our lives into yearly time units and to measure each year of age against each year's accomplishments. Between the age 20 and 30, we may expect—and often achieve—a 50 percent increase in our income, which exactly parallels our 50 percent increase in age. But since it is much less likely that our income will rise a further 66 percent between ages 30 and 50, it is this sense of diminishing returns with increasing age that turns the t-factor into an adversary during the middle age crisis.

3. *Continuous threat of defeat.* The *Wall Street Journal* has called attention to the pyramid effect in work life, meaning that there is more room at the bottom than at the top. Most of us, as members of a competitive society, have an unspoken awareness of this pyramid effect and, by middle adulthood, are likely to be disappointed over our position on the pyramid.

4. *Increase in dependency.* With increasing age generally come increasing responsibilities. To meet these demands, we must often turn to others for assistance—and render ourselves vulnerable to the results of their actions. As a 20-year-old, a salesman may rely on his own hard work to further his career. But as he moves up the pyramid and becomes a sales manager, he is dependent on the actions and skills of his subordinates to maintain his position. This may make him feel that he has lost direct control of his destiny—and contribute anxiety to the middle-age crisis.

5. *Denial of feelings.* By middle adulthood, many a person has become a member of what politicians, with some accuracy, call the silent majority. He has adapted himself to

society's rules of behavior and has learned to value the social virtues of politeness, dissimulation, and keeping one's thoughts to oneself. Yet in the course of a busy career, inevitable provocations bubble up for feelings of anger and guilt. What happens to these unexpressed feelings? Quite often, they surface in the form of psychosomatic complaints: ulcers, insomnia, headaches. A vicious cycle may then ensue, with these symptoms reinforcing the individual's sense of suddenly having aged considerably and his anxiety over aging causing additional sleeplessness, tension, and digestive upset.

6. *Constant state of defensiveness.* A dominant theme of that peculiarly American popular art form, the Western movie, has been the cocky young cowboy intending to challenge the aging but still skillful gunslinger. A similar battle between youth and maturity occurs daily in the more genteel precincts of the business and professional world. The middle adult must always be on his guard against challenges from talented young men and women with fresh ideas and a willingness to work for lower pay. This constant state of defensiveness, of decreasing security with increasing age, is a major factor in the middle-age crisis.

7. *Shift in prime-of-life concept.* For the fortunate and hard-working middle adult, success is attained in middle age following years of preparation and labor. For many middle adults, however, the fruits of success in the middle years have left a bitter taste. They feel that their prime of life has departed, unenjoyed, consumed in striving for the future. But now that the future has arrived, the middle adult may cast wistful glances back along his time frame to the psychological past.

The Success Neurosis

So success has not provided this middle adult with immunity against the stresses associated with this critical period.

In fact, many therapy patients have been observed to suffer from what is called *success neurosis* during the middle adult period. The person who is afflicted with this disorder has attained some much longed-for objective in life, yet suddenly —and for no apparent reason—begins to feel profoundly depressed.

There are several explanations for this paradoxical emotional reaction. First, consider the getting-there-is-half-the-fun principle. A person who spent years pursuing a certain goal —becoming a bank vice-president, a high school principal, a loading-dock foreman—has been immersed in the spirit of the hunt, the day to day details of advancement and progress. An air of excitement and adventurousness fills this pursuit, as well as considerable suspense. After 20 years of involvement with the means to an end, the achievement of that end may end the meaning of the individual's life. A natural letdown ensues, a negative reaction to success.

Another source of success neurosis is Dr. Martin Seligman's concept of depression as learned helplessness. When a person feels that his own actions have become irrelevant to the events in his life, he responds with a sense of depression rooted in impotence.

Powerful, successful individuals fit into this learned-helplessness paradigm by a process of unearned reward. During earlier stages of life, an individual sees his efforts translated directly into payoffs. If he works eight hours, he receives eight hours of pay. Having laid this groundwork for success, he is pleased—at first—to discover that he is now receiving greater payoffs for less effort. His business begins to run itself; his investments begin to pay dividends; his salary increases with longevity, even though he works no harder than before.

On one level, this is certainly pleasing. But on a deeper stratum, the sense that one's actions have become irrelevant to one's rewards is disturbing and depressing and feeds the success neurosis of middle adulthood.

In addition to marriage and work, the middle-adult time

bomb may also be detonated by family dispersion. A middle adult's children move away from home to weather independently their early adulthood crises. A middle adult's parents pass away. The middle adult male has become the family's elder statesman, and the middle adult female has become the keeper of an empty house, echoing with the ghostly cries of now grown children.

Viewed from this perspective, the impact of the middle adulthood time bomb is intimately bound up with the way a person views his or her time frame.

If he sees his psychological past as having consumed the bulk of what had once been an extensive psychological future, the time bomb of middle adulthood will hit with the force of an atomic explosion. But if the psychological future promises continued personal effectiveness, goal-seeking, and payoff-earning—experiences that complement and build on the contents of the psychological past—the shock waves of the middle adulthood time bomb are greatly muted and diminished.

Time Bomb IV: Late Adulthood

Improved medical care and preventive health measures have created an over-60 population explosion. Unfortunately, society's emphasis on youth and the shrinking number of tri-generational family units (households in which grandparents live with their children and grandchildren) have added fuel to the already explosive time bomb of late adulthood.

The time frame of the late adult is unique in one devastating respect, the disappearance of the psychological future. To the late adult, life begins to seem less of an ongoing process; more and more it becomes an almost-finished product. The late adult tends naturally to turn toward the psychological past with loaded questions: What have I done? What have I created? What am I leaving behind? This past-time orientation leads the late adult to speak frequently of the past, to savor old successes, nurse old grudges, repeat cautionary tales of pitfalls encountered or avoided.

While younger people frequently respond irritably to an old adult's penchant for reminiscence, there is evidence that the harvesting of the psychological past is a crucially rewarding service during this critical period of life.

Research in a New England nursing home illustrates this clearly. Psychologists tape-recorded the spontaneous conversation of a group of elderly men and women who were roughly the same age and in similar states of physical health. Some of these late adults tended to reminisce a great deal; others reminisced very little.

As years went by and nature pursued its inexorable course, all the subjects of this study died. The psychologists kept track of how many months each subject had lived following the study and obtained a startling result: The more a late adult had tended to reminisce, the longer he or she had lived. Those who had reminisced least had died soonest.

What can we make of these findings? Do late adults feed on their memories like that ancient symbol of time, the mythical serpent who devours his own tail? In a way, this does seem to happen. To reminisce, and receive attention to his reminiscences, the late adult has a fund of experiences accessibly stored in his psychological past. The richer his life has been, the greater his fund of reminiscence, and (as this experiment indicates) the longer the late adult may expect to live.

The likeliest explanation for the link between reminiscence and longevity seems to be that whoever is blessed with a psychological past dense with memorable experiences retains into late adulthood the capacity to enjoy life, past and present. His present will to live is stronger than that of a late adult with a sparse psychological past; and so his grip on life remains firmer.

So longevity is a product of psychological, as well as physical, factors. Proper exercise, nutrition, and medical care increase the probability of a long and healthy late adulthood, but how many of us also sense the importance of a psychological past well-furnished with experiences? Perhaps it is true that the more we have to look back on, the more time we will have to look forward to.

Sometimes, the late adult's grip on life can become a stifling force in the lives of his offspring. Out of a natural desire to feel useful, desirable, and valued, the late adult may impose himself on children or grandchildren. Or, in an attempt vicariously to relive events in the psychological past, the late adult may become an intrusive presence in the lives of descendants. Bitterness and resentment, volleyed between generational lines, may poison the relationships.

The late adult's attempt to "hijack" youth from younger relatives probably represents an attempt to avoid the awesome fact that late adulthood is life's final critical period. The future can now be reckoned in months and years, no longer in decades. Death, always an inescapable fact of life, may move into the present at any time.

Death is life's only example of absolute fair play: Everybody receives one death and nobody is overlooked. Until recently, death was a subject almost universally avoided. The dying person was so much a pariah that even his doctors tended to minimize contact with him. Recently, increasing attention has been focused on the emotional aspects of death and dying. A branch of medicine, *thanatology* (after Thanatos, the personification of death in Greek mythology), has been organized, and a professional journal, *Omega* (the final letter of the Greek alphabet), permits the dissemination of research into the subject of death as a psychological as well as physical process.

Hopefully, the elevation of death from a hidden and somewhat shameful phenomenon to its new status as a genuine crisis involving the individual's entire relationship to the t-factor during late adulthood will improve the quality of life during the final critical period. By focusing on death as an integral aspect of human experience, researchers may be able to illuminate and alleviate many of the still-secret stresses and strains that all of us may expect to experience in late adulthood.

15

Time Distortion

Consider a nightmare: You are taking a test required for promotion in your job. You have been told in advance that the test will begin at 9:00 A.M. and will end at noon. The questions are difficult, and you'll certainly need the entire three hours to finish. There is a large clock on the examination room's front wall. The test supervisor will use it to time the test. After scanning the questions, you begin to write. The clock indicates that it is 9:05.

In a few minutes, you look up and become aware that something strange is happening. The test supervisor has opened the clock and is moving its minute hand 60 full turns forward. The time now reads 10:10. You protest. The supervisor ignores you. He announces that only an hour and 50 minutes remains for the test.

Shaken, you resume work and pick up speed. When you again consult the clock, it shows the time as 9:16. He has turned it back again. You reduce your pace. Fifteen minutes later, the clock reads 11:25. You speed up desperately. A bell rings. You look up. The clock indicates that it is noon. You've hardly begun working on the test. You feel rooted to your seat. The bell continues to ring. It is your alarm clock. You awaken and escape from the nightmare.

Even if you've never experienced a nightmare remotely similar to the one I just described, you can probably grasp its terrifying quality. The nightmare is so frightening because it represents a world with one of your most important links to reality missing, the constancy of time, that reassuringly precise, even tick-tick-tick around which we organize our lives. We feel secure and reassured by the knowledge that one minute of clock time is neither longer nor shorter than any other.

But in the nightmare, time became distorted. Three hours no longer consisted of 180 minutes; they expanded and contracted at the whim of an unpredictable supervisor. Time was robbed of its most important quality, its constancy.

We take the constancy of time for granted. While our psychological pacemakers may be set at varying and variable tempos, we generally feel secure in the fact that time itself will unfold at a steady, even, and unvarying rate. I may feel that a three-hour test passes quite slowly, while you may perceive the three hours as having zipped by, but both of us take comfort in the fact that 180 minutes *feels* roughly like three hours to each of us.

Some individuals, however, lack this sense of t-factor constancy. They derive no comfort from the expectation that time will progress at a steady rate; the t-factor plays tricks on them, frightening tricks that confuse, confound, and disturb them with feelings similar to those depicted in our hypothetical nightmare. This chapter will examine some of the most common situations in which time becomes distorted and the t-factor runs wild.

When Memory Plays Tricks

Robert Wallis, a French-born physician now practicing in the United States, has suggested the apt phrase *temporal alienation* to describe the plight of someone who has lost his sense of time's constancy, usually because of some defect in brain function. Dr. Wallis notes that temporal alienation most often strikes the part of the time frame that we have called the psychological past. The temporally alienated person usually shows severe problems of memory. Some individuals, for example, may suffer from *ecmnesia*. In this type of temporal alienation, events that occurred in the past are hallucinated in the present: The individual feels that he is experiencing them now.

Others, often those suffering from brain damage due to chronic alcoholism, display *confabulation*. A confabulator has a very poor memory for recent events. Rather than saying, "I don't remember what I did last night," he invents a story, often quite implausible, to fill the gap in his psychological past.

A patient hospitalized with Korsakoff's psychosis, a disease related to nutritional deficiency caused by years of excessive alcohol intake, once reported to his doctor that his daughter had taken him to a restaurant the night before. He described the meal and recounted an argument with his daughter. On checking, the doctor discovered that the patient had not been away from the hospital in weeks and that his daughter lived 2000 miles away.

A third group of patients report the feeling that all their current experiences occurred previously. The present is a repetition of the psychological past. Most of us, to a much more limited degree, also experience this feeling at times. We call it déjà vu (French for "already seen"). Perhaps because it is a type of temporal alienation that normal people experience as well as impaired patients, déjà vu has attracted much interest.

Charles Dickens, a man with scientific as well as literary talent, provided the best description of déjà vu in writing:

We have all some experience of a feeling which comes over us occasionally, of what we are saying and doing have been said and done before, in a remote time—or of having been surrounded, dim ages ago, by the same faces, objects, and circumstances—often knowing perfectly what will be said next, as if we suddenly remembered it.

Scientific explanations of déjà vu have followed two separate pathways. Some researchers feel that déjà vu experiences are a means by which a person may deal with anxiety. Others believe that it results from faulty brain functioning.

Dr. Louis Linn, a psychiatrist on the faculty of Mt. Sinai Medical School in New York, supports the anxiety-control view of déjà vu. According to Dr. Linn, "Implicit in the feeling 'I have experienced this before' is the reassuring further thought 'and I survived in spite of my fears.' " He compares such experiences to a common dream, similar to the nightmare we considered earlier, called an examination dream.

In an examination dream, the dreamer is confronted by a difficult life challenge, an interview or test. During the dream he seems to be doing very poorly in meeting the challenge and feels quite anxious. But when he wakes up, he realizes that he's really been dreaming about a challenge that he confronted and successfully mastered in the past. The meaning of the dream, then, is: You may be anxious now, but remember how well you did before. Which is why Dr. Linn thinks that examination dreams as well as déjà vu experiences are methods of controlling anxieties.

Another View of Déjà Vu

The alternate view is represented by Dr. Robert Efron of the Neurophysiology-Biophysics Research Unit at the Boston Veterans Administration Hospital. The basis for Dr. Efron's theory of déjà vu is that our brains consist of two halves (hemispheres), which are equal in size but function quite differently. The dominant hemisphere, usually the left, is in control of language, speech, and time-labeling (our sense of *when* things happen). The nondominant hemisphere serves important nonverbal functions, primarily the perception of pace. The hemispheres are linked by a thick cable of nerve fibers so they can transmit messages to each other.

When we have a new experience—let's say we walk into an unfamiliar room—our sense organs report this experience to both halves of our brain. When the sensations from our sense organs directly reach the dominant half of the brain, they are registered. When they reach the nondominant half of the brain they are instantaneously transmitted through the nerve cable to the dominant half. When the brain is functioning correctly, the two sensations arrive simultaneously and are simultaneously registered in the dominant hemisphere. We say, "Here I am in an unfamiliar room."

But suppose there is a delay in transmission of the experience from the nondominant to the dominant brain hemisphere. Our experience of entering the room flows with the dominant hemisphere directly from the sense again and then—after a second's delay—*again* enters the dominant hemisphere from the other side of the brain. This causes the experience to be registered twice, and we have the uncanny feeling that we've entered the room before.

"Under these conditions," Dr. Efron suggests, "a person might have the following rapid but unconscious interpretation: 'Everything I am perceiving *now* has already occurred once before (because it has already been logged-in by the left hemisphere via the direct pathway).' "

Dr. Efron offers persuasive evidence to support his theory. He points out that patients with damage to the nondominant brain hemisphere frequently report déjà vu experiences. Presumably, their brain damage delays the indirect transmission of experiences and causes sensation to be registered twice by the dominant hemisphere. Also, it is quite common for persons diagnosed as epileptic to have déjà vu feelings just before a seizure occurs. The storm of electrical activity brewing in the epileptic's brain presumably disrupts and delays communication between brain hemispheres and causes experiences to be reported twice. So when Dickens wrote that déjà vu is a feeling "of knowing perfectly what will be said next, as if we suddenly remembered it," he was quite correct in a sense. But we do not remember the experience from the dim past, as Dickens believed; we remember it from the recent past when it was first registered, just a few seconds earlier.

Since most of us are fortunate enough to possess well-functioning brains, it may be that occasional déjà vu experiences arise from transient bursts of electrical activity that momentarily disrupt the simultaneous deluge of messages from the nondominant hemisphere. And in anxiety-producing situations, we may indeed, as Dr. Linn suggests, employ déjà vu as a means of self-reassurance.

When I discussed the t-factor dysfunctions that arise from damage to the brain caused by alcoholism and other diseases that attack the nervous system, I mentioned the crucial role played by the brain in our ability to perceive time. Scientists have not been satisfied, however, merely to note the connection between brain impairments and t-factor distortions. They have wondered whether some parts of the brain are more sensitive to the t-factor than others.

Two Israeli researchers, Dr. Amiram Carmon and Dr. Israel Nechson, studied 47 patients at Hadassah Hospital in Jerusalem. Roughly half of the patients suffered from damage to the left hemisphere; the remaining patients had impairments in the right hemisphere. Each patient was given a test consisting of sequences of lights and sounds. After each sequence, the subject was asked to report in what order the stimuli had been presented: which came first, second, third, and so forth. In this way the researchers could discover how their subjects differed in the ability to order their experiences in terms of time.

The two groups differed significantly. Patients with damage to the left side of the brain performed much more poorly than those with right-hemisphere damage. In fact, the patients with right-sided damage did almost as well as a 42-member control group with no brain damage at all. This study demonstrated with great clarity the fact that it's the left, or dominant, hemisphere of the brain that enables us to perceive, understand, and benefit from the t-factor. When the left hemisphere is impaired, temporal alienation occurs.

T-Factor Distortions

Unfortunately, individuals afflicted with brain disorders are not the only people for whom the t-factor runs wild. Difficulties with time perception, sometimes mild, often severe, also occur in many people who suffer from various psychiatric illness. This is not surprising. After all, since time is an important factor in day-to-day living, we might expect that individuals with serious problems in day-to-day living would have difficulties with the t-factor.

Such t-factor distortions are seen most strikingly in men and women who are diagnosed as schizophrenic. Schizophrenia is a psychic disorder that disrupts thought processes and social relationships. It may take a variety of forms: withdrawal from social contacts with other people; hallucination of voices; emotional unresponsiveness; false belief that one is being talked about, spied upon, or controlled by others; and inability to concentrate or to think logically. While schizophrenics are a remarkably diverse group of people, years of research with chronic schizophrenics have demonstrated that these patients often display difficulties in thinking and perception, so psychologists have been interested in learning how schizophrenia affects an individual's relationship to the t-factor.

Inconsistency is the keynote of the schizophrenic's ability to perceive time. Psychologist Albert Rabin, working with a group of schizophrenic patients, found that some of them consistently and wildly overestimated brief spans of time; others tended greatly to underestimate; and some swung giddily between the two extremes. Clearly lacking in these individuals was a firm grasp upon the constancy of time that is so necessary to smooth functioning in daily life.

Other psychologists discovered that schizophrenics have an extremely limited sense of the psychological future. They find it difficult to anticipate events that have not yet occurred. When asked to put future events in their proper sequence—for example, New Year's Day, 1979, the next presidential election, or the expiration of a driver's license—schizophrenics often respond in a confused manner. The lack of t-factor control in these patients suggests that their experience of the world possesses many of the terrifying features of the nightmare I described earlier.

A therapist who works with schizophrenic patients is often startled by time distortions that arise in the course of therapy. One psychiatrist had been treating a schizophrenic patient for five years without any appreciable improvement. The psychiatrist asked his patient whether his lack of progress caused him to feel frustrated. "Frustrated?" responded the patient. "No, not after such a short time." Surprised, the psychiatrist asked the patient how long they'd been working together. "Three months," said the patient, "four maybe. I've lost count. But there's plenty more time left in the clock."

This patient displayed a form of t-factor distortion that is sometimes called timelessness. In such cases, it is not so much a matter of the schizophrenic perceiving time incorrectly; he is attempting to ignore—or escape from—time completely. One possible motivation for this t-factor escapism may be the schizophrenic's frequently very concrete approach to abstract notions like time. He attempts to reduce the concept of time to a simple term that he can grasp. When the patient commented, "There's plenty of time left in the clock," for instance, he displayed this sort of concreteness, translating time into something physically consumable, like coal in a bin, or groceries on a shelf.

The schizophrenic's concrete approach to time explains one

common example of schizophrenic timelessness: extreme boredom. A schizophrenic patient in a modern psychiatric hospital is surrounded by any number of opportunities for work, recreation, and therapy. Occupational therapists invite him to acquire typing skills or clerical abilities; recreation therapists encourage him to participate in sports and leisure-time activities; social workers and nurses involve him in group therapy seminars. Amidst all this activity, if you ask the schizophrenic how he feels, he is likely to reply, "Bored."

Some professionals believe that boredom is not really a problem for the schizophrenic; it is a strategy he uses to cope with his fear that time is slipping away from him. By cultivating a sense of timelessness, the schizophrenic is able to reassure himself that he is not losing time by using it. With primitive logic, the schizophrenic reasons that time can be spent and saved, like money. If he's bored, he cannot be spending time in activities; he must be saving it—and thereby prolonging his life.

We can see that one crucial element in schizophrenia is the inability to separate emotional fears and conflicts from the process of thinking and perception. A fascinating experiment conducted by a team of two psychologists at Michigan State University, Drs. David R. Pearl and Paul Berg, revealed how this inability causes the schizophrenic to perceive time in a distorted way. The psychologists studied three groups, each composed of 16 schizophrenic patients. One group had great difficulty in handling sexual feelings; the second group had aggressive conflicts and feelings of anger; and the third group's major conflict was in their feelings of dependency.

The psychologists reasoned that each patient would have the most difficulty in identifying time when exposed to a situation which would spark his major emotional conflict. To test this hypothesis, they showed each patient four pictures: three were designed to arouse either sexual, angry, or dependent feelings; and one was to be an entirely neutral picture. The sexual picture showed a woman wearing a flimsy nightgown;

the aggressive picture showed a huge man with clenched fists about to strike an unsuspecting smaller man; the dependency picture showed a weak-looking man in a room with an older woman; and the neutral picture showed a boat beside a stream.

Each picture was flashed at four speeds—5, 10, 20, and 30 seconds—and the patients were asked to judge how long each one had remained on the screen. The results were conclusive. Patients with sexual conflicts distorted time more when shown the sexual picture. Patients with aggressive conflicts displayed similar t-factor distortion when they were shown the aggressive picture. And those with dependency conflicts tended to distort time when they viewed the dependency picture. The neutral picture evoked much less t-factor distortion in all groups. It seems clear that schizophrenics have difficulty in separating feelings from their ability to perceive time. When disturbing feelings were aroused, t-factor distortions increased.

It is not surprising that schizophrenics are often described as emotionally blunted or socially unresponsive. This flattening of emotions and shrinking from social contact minimizes the chances that unpleasant feelings will be aroused and cause distortions in thinking and perception.

In self-defense, the schizophrenic seems to "tune out" much of the environment, and this tuning-out process leads to further difficulties in dealing with the t-factor. Healthy individuals perceive time by paying attention to cues provided by the environment. You can tell by a number of clues that a movie lasting 120 minutes is longer than one lasting 40 minutes: fatigue, hunger, thirst, the number of events that occurred in each movie, etc. The schizophrenic shuts himself off from such clues. Research conducted in New York by Drs. William Lhamon and Sanford Goldstone has demonstrated that a schizophrenic's ability to distort time arises directly from his failing to utilize the t-factor information that is available to him.

Time distortion, then, is an important feature of schizophrenia and an example of how severely the schizophrenic individual may be cut off from the world of reality and t-factor constancy.

To a much more limited degree, neurotic people who maintain much closer contact with reality may also experience t-factor distortion. Quite frequently, a neurotically depressed person may report that "time has slowed down to a crawl." One depressed patient reported, "I can't remember the last morning; yesterday is as remote as events years ago." A similar feeling was presented by another patient, who said, "Everything I have done seems like a long time ago; when evening comes, and I think back over the day, it seems years away."

These comments typify the t-factor distortion that frequently troubles seriously depressed people. The depressive becomes a tortoise to time's hare, plodding sadly along with a psychological pacemaker ticking ever so slowly. This slowing in the depressive's experience of time is reflected in other areas of his life as well. Depressed people often display motor retardation, a considerable slowness in making any movements more vigorous than a sigh. Even the bodily processes slow down during depression. The digestive system contracts at a reduced rate, leading to weight loss and the depressed person's frequent complaint that he is constipated.

Psychologists have naturally been interested in learning whether the depressed individual's feeling that time has slowed down is related to an actual distortion in his ability to perceive the t-factor. To answer this question, Drs. Alexander Mezey and Samuel Cohen of the Maudsley Hospital in London studied 12 men and 9 women suffering from neurotic depression. Most of the patients reported that time seemed to have slowed down for them. Each patient was asked to estimate a 30-second interval while depressed and then again after he was discharged from the hospital.

The results were not clear-cut. When depressed, the patients did seem somewhat slowed in their sense of time, reporting on average that 30 seconds felt more like 40 seconds. But after discharge from the hospital, their accuracy did not improve significantly; 30 seconds now felt like 35 seconds on average. It is possible, of course, that the patients hadn't completely recovered from depression when retested on discharge. This would explain why their sense of time remained relatively slow. Also, thirty seconds may not have been a long enough period of time to reflect a true slowing of the psychological pacemaker.

If a depressed person feels like a tortoise to time's hare, it seems fair to wonder whether an extremely anxious individual senses that time is passing so quickly that he feels like a hare to time's tortoise. Anxiety increases the rate of such bodily functions as heartbeat and respiration, and so it might be expected to speed up the sense of time as well. Drs. Cohen and Mezey tested this notion by asking 24 doctors who were about to speak in public to estimate a 30-second interval. They compared the accuracy of these t-factor estimations to estimates that were made when the same doctors were relaxed. No differences were found, a surprising result that may have occurred because the doctors were not neurotically anxious but merely mildly anxious. Indeed, when a researcher at the University of Maryland Medical School, Dr. Aron Siegman gave a time-estimation test to 36 subjects, some of whom were extremely anxious, he found that the more anxious the subject was, the faster time seemed to pass for him.

T-Factor Dropouts

The t-factor distortions experienced by schizophrenics and depressed and anxious people shared one quality: unpleasantness. If offered a choice, all would opt for a return of the ability to perceive time clearly, for a chance to tame the wildness of the t-factor. But a large and growing group of people actively seek t-factor distortion and cultivate t-factor wildness. These are the t-factor dropouts.

What is there in the dropout's relationship to the t-factor

that impels him to seek escape from it? Dr. Franklin S. Du-
Bois of the Silver Hill Foundation in New Canaan, Connecticut, has attempted to answer this question by exploring the
symbolic significance that time holds for many people.

According to Dr. DuBois, time is one of our most powerful
symbols of authority. We live by the clock. Speed and punctuality are virtues. Slowness and lateness are vices. At work, we
are accountable for our hours; many of us punch a time clock
twice a day. If one person must account to another person how
his time is spent, he is in an inferior and subordinate relationship to that person. Freedom is the ability to spend time as one
chooses, but each of us is imprisoned in one sort of schedule
or another.

Dr. DuBois believes that individuals who have difficulty in
dealing with the authority figures in their lives experience a
corresponding difficulty with the t-factor because it symbolizes
authority. He notes that people who perceived their parents as
arbitrary, interfering, and critical are likely to rebel against all
authority figures. So they rebel against time as well. It is no
coincidence that one of the most popular symbols of the
t-factor is Father Time.

If the t-factor dropout's desire to escape the control and
constancy of time can be interpreted as a wish to rebel against
authority in general, how is this rebellion accomplished? Perhaps the most popular escape route from the t-factor has been
provided by the smoking of marijuana. Dr. Lester Grinspon, a
Harvard psychiatrist, has intensively studied the psychological
effects of marijuana. While he found little evidence that mari-
juana-smoking causes serious impairment in thinking or perception, he observes that time distortion is frequently reported
by marijuana users; they feel that "ten minutes seem like an
hour."

Musicians feel that they are able to cram more notes into a
given span of time while smoking marijuana; so when they are
high, they enjoy what seems to be a greater sense of freedom
from the dictates of clock time. An anonymous psychologist
described his own experience with marijuana and agreed that

it seemed to provide escape from time limits. "One of the effects of marijuana," he discovered, "is to reduce the strength of expectancies and goals which are socially reinforced. Nontime experiences are increased in relative strength and time-oriented associations are decreased, which creates the sense that time is expanded."

You may have noticed a similarity between the t-factor dropout's attitude toward time and the schizophrenic's sense of timelessness. In both cases, the individual has escaped the authority imposed by time, and rebels against the fact that time is apportioned to each of us in limited quantities. The difference, of course, is that the marijuana smoker actively seeks his t-factor distortion; the schizophrenic seems to have fallen into his timeless state involuntarily.

The more powerful psychedelic drugs, particularly LSD, probably provide the t-factor dropout with time distortions and other perceptual distortions similar to those experienced by schizophrenics. On LSD trips, according to psychologist Frank Barron, "the passage of time may seem to be a slow and pleasant flow or to be intolerably tedious." So in escaping from the authority of time, the LSD user may seek the pleasurable expansion of time attained by the marijuana smoker, but may find instead the empty, endless timelessness experienced by the schizophrenic.

Meditation Makes Time Crawl

A third major escape route from the constancy of time is probably the oldest and also the newest tool employed by the t-factor dropout: meditation. Throughout history, mystical practices have been traditional in many societies. The keynote has generally been the ability to alter bodily functions through purely mental processes. Recent research on individuals able to enter such altered states of consciousness has revealed that successful meditation involves a voluntary slowing down of the brain's electrical activity until a pattern of languorous alpha brain waves is achieved. Since other biological processes tend to slow down as an alpha state is achieved, it is reasonable also to anticipate a slowing in the sense of time.

Reports obtained from successful meditations confirm this anticipation, as does psychological research. One investigator studied eight research subjects whom he taught to meditate. Each subject was instructed to focus his attention on a blue vase and to ignore all other stimulation. To test the strength of meditative powers, the researcher piped tape-recorded music and poetry into the room, but the subjects were able to filter out all sounds by centering their attention strictly on the blue vase.

After a long meditation session, the investigator questioned each subject about his subjective experiences. There was unanimous agreement that the sense of time had slowed considerably during meditation. All the subjects believed that the session had been quite brief and were surprised to learn how lengthy it actually had been. Meditation, then, seems to offer a nonchemical means of escape from t-factor constancy for those who seek time distortion without potential side effects.

Is it coincidental that the greatest interest in marijuana smoking, LSD, and meditation has come from adolescents? Almost certainly not. You'll recall that the hallmark of adolescence is rebellion against the psychological past and anxiety about the psychological future, so it's not surprising that t-factor dropouts cluster within this age group. Much of the puzzling behavior that typifies adolescence—which has been called the temporary schizophrenic period of life—may be understood as an attempt to achieve freedom, through t-factor distortion, from authority symbolized by time.

T-Factor Modification

While time distortions can be imposed by illness and cultivated by anyone longing for a vacation from t-factor constancy, there is a third important sense of time distortion:

t-factor modification, meaning one person's attempts to alter another person's ability to perceive time. Most commonly, t-factor modification is achieved through hypnotism.

An experiment performed by Herbert Krauss, Raymond Katzell, and Beatrice Krauss at Hunter College in New York demonstrates how hypnotism can bring one individual's sense of time under another person's control. The researchers hypnotized ten subjects and gave them the hypnotic suggestion that three minutes would go by so slowly that they would seem more like ten minutes. Once this suggestion had been accepted, each subject received a list of 60 words and was told to memorize as many as possible. A control group of subjects was given the same list, but had a full ten minutes of clock time to learn them.

After three minutes of clock time had passed, the hypnotized group was tested to see how many words they could recall. After ten minutes the control group was similarly tested. Remarkably, the three-minute group learned just as many words as the ten-minute group. Apparently, the hypnotic time-slowing suggestion had effectively altered the subjects' sense of time to the point that they were able to cram ten minutes' worth of learning into three minutes.

Hypnotic age regression is another example of t-factor modification. While in a hypnotic state, some individuals have received the suggestion that they have traveled backward and returned to an earlier stage of life in the psychological past. A person regressed under hypnosis to the age of five may speak in a childish voice and make bodily movements typical of a five-year-old.

Some critics of the age regression notion have suggested that a person may not really be returning to an early life but may merely be offering an adult's imitation of childish behavior. In response to this challenge the research team of Robert R. Reiff and Martin Scheerer performed a classic age-regression experiment. They hypnotized subjects, suggested that they regress to an earlier age, and then gave the subjects psychological tests. The test results indicated that the subjects

168 PART THREE: *Time Traps, Bombs, and Distortions*

were using modes of thought typical of childhood and virtually impossible to imitate by an adult. In addition, Reiff and Scheerer asked each subject for specific details—the names of grade school teachers, for example—that the subjects had not been able to recall before age regression. By checking their subjects' replies against their school records, the researchers confirmed that they had indeed returned to an earlier stage of life.

While age regression may seem at first glance to be an amusing psychological parlor game, this form of t-factor modification may become a powerful tool for treating emotional distress. A psychiatrist, Margaret Bowers, has demonstrated the therapeutic potential of age regression in her treatment of a troubled musician. When the patient entered therapy he was too anxiety-ridden to earn a living. He couldn't even audition for jobs. Dr. Bowers felt that his past experiences significantly influenced his present difficulties, but the musician was unable to shed much light on his history.

Using hypnotic age regression, Dr. Bowers returned the patient to his psychological past. While hypnotized, he relived a series of extremely traumatic experiences including sex-play with his father and the witnessing of sexual contact between his parents. He had devoted so much of his energy to defending himself against these powerful memories that he had become quite unable to function as an adult. These experiences, retrieved by hypnotic age regression, enabled Dr. Bowers to help her patient work through and overcome the traumatic contents of his psychological past.

T-factor modification is the most positive of the three major t-factor distortions I have discussed in this chapter because it represents a process of seeking and practical helping, not escaping and avoiding.

Nobody Is Immune to Time Distortion

Happily, few of us are schizophrenic or chronically depressed or anxious. We may sometimes chafe at the authority symbolized by time but we do not become t-factor dropouts. We perform like good sports and quack like a duck in response to the suggestion of a stage-hypnotist, but we probably never have or never will experience hypnotic age regression. Can we then consider ourselves immune to time distortion?

No. To a (fortunately mild) degree, everyone's t-factor goes somewhat wild on occasion. For biological or psychological reasons, your sense of time constancy can slip.

Fatigue is probably the most common cause. If you've ever driven for hours on a straight highway through an unchanging landscape or total darkness, you probably noticed how frequently you checked the time and how impressed you were at its slow passage. The monotony of your surroundings, combined with the physical stress of sitting in one place exerts a distorting effort on your perception of time.

A psychologist, Harold Gulliksen investigated the effect of fatigue on time perception by giving 320 subjects eight different activities to perform. They ranged in tediousness from passively resting the head on folded arms to taking down dictation. Each activity lasted exactly 200 seconds and subjects were asked to estimate the duration of each. Gulliksen found that the most time distortion occurred during activities that were either extremely tiring (like taking rapid dictation) or extremely boring (doing nothing).

Psychological factors also seem to play an important part in everyday time distortion, primarily factors that influence perception. While we noted earlier that a schizophrenic has great difficulty in separating his emotions from his perceptions, healthy individuals can also experience perceptual distortions.

If a person is hungry and a series of three words—*mile, milk,* and *mill*—is flashed very quickly before his eyes, he is likely to recognize the word *milk* the soonest. After lunch, however, there will be no difference in his threshold of perception. If a prudish individual is exposed to the three words *rock, cock,* and *lock* at decreasing speeds, he is likely to perceive the middle word last of the three. Our perceptions are influenced by our emotional needs.

170 PART THREE: *Time Traps, Bombs, and Distortions*

In the same way, t-factor needs can create distortions in time perception. Two University of Pennsylvania psychologists, Robert Filer and Donald Meals, wondered whether an individual's need for time to pass quickly could cause him to experience a t-factor distortion. They performed two experiments with college students.

In the first, they told students in a class that they could be excused immediately after completing a tedious 10-minute task. In another class, a control group of students were given the same task but not told they would be excused. After 4 minutes and 37 seconds, the students were asked to estimate how much time had gone by. Those who were to be excused upon completion of the task estimated that 5½ minutes had passed; the control group estimated that only 4¾ minutes had elapsed. In the second experiment, the researchers offered a new group of students a prize after completing a 10-minute task. When stopped after 4 minutes and 37 seconds, this group again thought that 5½ minutes had gone by, while control subjects again estimated the elapsed time accurately.

These experiments revealed how powerfully our needs can distort our perception of time. When we want time to pass by rapidly, this wish can interfere with accurate perception of time and speed up the sense of its passing.

We can also shift into reverse and, when facing a dreaded event, slow down our time sense. The waiting room phenomenon, seen every day in dentists' offices around the country, is a case in point. While waiting to see the dentist, many of us wish that time would decelerate if not stop completely. If we arrive a half hour early for the appointment, we sit reading a magazine for what feels like five minutes and are thunderstruck to check our watch and see that twenty minutes have already passed. Just as the college students were disappointed to learn that they were not as close to finishing their test as their estimated time sense had led them to believe they were, we are chagrined to discover that we are closer in time than we had believed to sitting in that feared dentist's chair.

In both cases—and in other activity of daily life too numerous to detail—our human sense of time's constancy can become distorted by emotional needs and fears. Fortunately, a healthy individual's t-factor goes wild only on occasion, is quickly brought back under control, and provides one of the most important links to reality and stability in our lives.

Part Four

TUNING YOUR
TIME MACHINE

16

The Crime of Wasted Time

The t-factor is an extremely flexible force in your life. You may spend time or save it, waste time or borrow it, steal time or juggle it. These activities have positive or negative effects but they all focus attention on one central question: How do you *use* the t-factor in your life?

The quality of your life, your sense of self-fulfillment vs. self-dissatisfaction, is directly determined by your answer to this question. To the extent that you use time productively, the quality of your life is enhanced; to the degree that you abuse the t-factor, the quality of your life is diminished. So how do you allocate, or possibly misallocate, that scarcest of your natural resources: the t-factor?

Wasted Time and its Antidotes

Your definition of wasted time is probably different from that of other people. Almost everybody would agree that certain activities are clearly time-wasters—blackening in all the letter *O*s on this page, for example—but even such obvious cases are open to some doubt.

A psychologist once conducted an experiment with one

group of subjects who were paid to black in all the *O*s on a number of pages and another group who performed the task without payment. He then asked each subject how much he or she had enjoyed the task and found that the unpaid subjects enjoyed it more than the paid subjects. This indicated that an individual who doesn't receive a tangible reward for an unpleasant task tends to compensate by adopting a more favorable attitude toward the task. In light of this useful result, the subjects who blacked in the *O*s did not waste their time; they contributed to science.

The definition of wasted time must therefore be subjective. It should come from within you. It would be helpful for you to list below two or three ways in which you feel that your t-factor is currently being wasted. Use the following definition as a guide: A time-waster is any activity that you engage in regularly and which does not benefit you either psychologically, emotionally, financially, socially, or intellectually.

Next to each time-waster listed, write your estimate, in minutes or hours, of how much of your t-factor it absorbs each day. By adding up these estimates, you will obtain a useful notion of the degree to which you are misallocating your t-factor.

Time Wasters	Daily Amount
1.	
2.	
3.	_____

Daily Wasted Time =

There is no lack of systems designed to cut down wasted time. In work settings and personal life, many have proved to be useful. One of the most charming systems was proposed by the English novelist Arnold Bennett in a book ambitiously titled *How to Live on 24 Hours a Day*.

Bennett believed passionately in the t-factor as a natural resource. Time, according to Bennett, is the inexplicable raw material of everything. With it, all is possible; without it, nothing. The supply of time is truly a daily miracle, an affair genuinely astonishing, when we examine it. You wake up in the morning, and lo! your purse is magically filled with twenty-four hours of the unmanufactured time of the universe of your life! It is yours. It is the most precious of possessions.

Bennett's suggestions for extracting maximum benefits from your purseful of time were less ambitious than his book's title implies. He restricted his focus to "a day within a day" consisting of the nonworking hours, roughly between 5:00 P.M. and 9:00 A.M. Dropping an eight-hour sleep period left eight daily hours of "living" time. He further whittled this period down to a half-hour of commuting time six mornings a week plus 90 minutes three evenings a week. So his program might more honestly have been titled *How to Live on 7½ Hours a Week*.

But Bennett's notions of how these 7½ hours might profitably be used were definite and constructive. He began by banning newspaper reading during each morning's commuting time. What to do with the three weekly hours thus conserved? Bennett suggested that you embark on a program of "mind control": Concentrate on one specific subject for a half hour each morning. You might choose to reflect on a book you've been reading, an historical period that fascinates you, or a psychological topic of interest. (Time psychology perhaps?) What you choose to concentrate on is less important than the fact that you are centering your attention on one subject, resisting all distractions and extraneous thoughts. If your concentration wanders, Bennett enjoins, "Bring it back by the scruff of the neck."

The benefits of such mental sitting-up exercises each morning are undeniable and Bennett seems, in fact, to have anticipated the more recent trend to which many executives and professionals subscribe: to begin the day with some routine

that centers on the self. Commuting time is thereby transformed from a tedious waiting period to a time of productive
intellectual activity.

As to evening time, Bennett points out that most of us are
not as tired after a hard day's work as we think. The feeling
of fatigue is more likely one of boredom from lack of stimulation offered by the usual evening routines. He suggests a study
program for his three 90-minute segments: serious reading,
lecture attendance, or active learning in one field. Such a program provides a regular, scheduled method for converting
previously wasted time into time well spent. Although Bennett
made these suggestions more than half a century B.T. (before
television), they seem relevant and psychologically useful today and require little disruption of your daily activities.

By restricting his attention to a mere seven and a half hours
each week, Bennett obviously ignored that other large tracts
of the t-factor may be wasted. Modern methods for reducing
wasted time also devote intense attention to the efficient allocation of time during your work day. These systems emphasize
the importance of identifying repetitious activities that may
drain hours from your daily allocation of the t-factor and of
listing priorities so you can schedule time efficiently.

While such systems have proved useful in many industries,
they share one common drawback: They are too general.
They assume that most t-factor waste is the result of poor
scheduling, so they propose to solve such problems with general suggestions to help you develop more efficient time
schedules. But our interest is your time as you experience it individually, and so I will explain the specific psychological
factors that may lead *you* to waste time.

Time Hoarding and Mortgaging

I know a man who is a time hoarder. He deals with the
t-factor like cigar lovers in the days prior to the embargo on

trade with Cuba. Just as tobaccophiles laid in enormous stocks of their precious Havanas in preparation for the leaner days to come, the time hoarder attempts to squirrel away huge chunks of his psychological future to draw upon if the need ever arises.

How does he accomplish this feat? Let him tell it:

> At the start of every month, I make up a list of all the things I know I'll have to do. Pay the rent and other bills, do the laundry, shop for clothing, service the car, do my business bookkeeping, and so on. Once I have the list prepared, I try to complete all these items during the first week of the month. Then I have three weeks free and clear, loaded with time to spend as I choose, not as I have to.

During the first week of each month, naturally, the time hoarder is a blur of frenetic activity. His friends can rarely reach him by telephone. In fact, to minimize distractions from his self-imposed burden of telescoping a full month's tasks into a single week, he often leaves his telephone off the hook. He is self-employed and therefore free to absent himself from his office when his taskmaster list dictates. An answering service takes his calls; unfortunately, it cannot literally answer them, so new business must wait. He declines most social engagements scheduled for Week No. 1. His excuse is simple and honest, "I just don't have the time."

The time hoarder is similar to those eccentrics who live in poverty but are discovered when they die to have thousands of dollars secreted in a mattress. In an attempt to build up an undepletable stock of the t-factor, the time hoarder deprives himself of the pleasures associated with spending time, just as the miserly eccentric cackles impecuniously over his cache of money. Like other hoarders, the time hoarder sacrifices the past to the future.

The time hoarder objects to this comparison and points out

that he has the choice of spending his amassed treasure trove of time during three weeks of the month out of four. But somehow, his acquaintances have observed, this spending rarely seems to take place. Following a variation of Parkinson's famous law—tasks arise to absorb all available time—the time hoarder's three weeks usually confront him with a multitude of chores he had never anticipated, more dull "must do" activities that act like inflationary prices in whittling down the value of his t-factor holdings. And as each month begins the time hoarder gamely resumes his futile attempt to snare that elusive quarry: free time.

Other people adopt the opposite attitude toward the t-factor. They are time mortgagers, and their technique was used by Napoleon Bonaparte. It is said that whenever Napoleon received a letter, he put it aside unread for two weeks. After two weeks, he observed, most of the problems raised by the letters resolved themselves. After this t-factor filtering, Napoleon could then address himself to the few problems still unsolved.

The time mortgager sacrifices the future to the present. His t-factor strategy is one of postponement. One patient, a confirmed time mortgager, summed up the essence of this strategy by saying, "When I put off an unpleasant chore for a week or two, I think to myself, 'If the world comes to an end this week, or if I'm hit by a truck on Friday, that's one annoying thing I never had to do.' "

The time hoarder and the time mortgager seem poles apart, the former saving time's capital for use on a sunny day that never quite materializes, and the latter borrowing time in the hope that future events will somehow permit him to default on the loan. But in an important sense these opposites are similar. Both maintain a skewed (or lopsided) relationship to the t-factor. The hoarder is skewed toward the future; the mortgager toward the present. The one engages in a t-factor fast, the other in a t-factor feast, but neither attains a sound, productive level of t-factor consumption. So the hoarder and the mortgager are partners in a psychological crime: the crime of wasted time.

Killing Time Is an Aggressive Act

If you were to set fire to a ten dollar bill, your behavior would be considered peculiar in the extreme. You'd be attacking your financial resources for no good reason and robbing yourself of ten dollars. Yet when you engage in the similar form of self-robbing popularly known as killing time, no one gives it a second thought. After all, doesn't everyone kill time now and then?

Perhaps. But ask yourself one question: Who are you killing when you kill time, when you procrastinate, delay, or put off what needs to be done? Some investigators believe that time killing is a form of symbolic aggression, hostility that you divert toward figures in your life whom you perceive as controlling and authoritative. As Dr. Joost Meerloo has noted, "Man is caught up in scheduling from the moment of his birth. Time and schedule symbolize the compelling and intruding forces that offered man's infantile feeling of omnipotence."

One patient whose emotional problems centered on the inability to make proper use of the t-factor is a good example. Though she was extremely well-intentioned, she seemed unable to hold a job. While employed as a door-to-door saleswoman of cosmetic products, she frequently took three-hour lunches and went to movies for the balance of the afternoon. Soon her poor sales resulted in dismissal.

She was killing time and time-killing was destroying her career. As her treatment progressed, it became apparent that she harbored tremendous and unexpressed feelings of hostility toward her parents, an extremely controlling couple. These aggressive feelings were transferred onto any person in a position of authority over the patient. In childhood, her teachers had been exasperated by her failure to produce assignments on time. As she entered the vocational world, her hostility toward employers came out in the form of lateness, nonperformance, lack of initiative, and—killing time.

This woman was killing time as a symbolic substitute for directly expressing her hostility toward her parents. When her hostility was worked through in treatment—which later was extended to family therapy—she became increasingly able to use, rather than kill, her daily allotment of the t-factor.

Similarly, a child who holds his breath until he turns blue expresses anger toward his parents by hurting himself. In some cultures, an individual expresses anger by committing suicide on a hated enemy's doorstep; this is killing time pushed to its furthest extreme: The suicidal individual is literally destroying all the time remaining in his life and blaming his enemy for the act.

Other forms of time-killing are common in our society, less self-destructive and more directly aggressive. Keeping somebody waiting is frequently an expression of hostility: You are killing *his* time. Conversely, when you are kept waiting, you may feel rejected and victimized. This sort of waiting game occurs often in telephone contacts between executives and professionals, or, more likely, between their secretaries. The object of the game is to induce one party to wait, holding a silent telephone, until the other party comes on the line. The amount of time one party is compelled to waste becomes an index of his lower ranking in relation to the other.

How much of your t-factor is wasted in an expression of hostility? Are you always late or excessively prompt? Punctuality carried to extremes is, surprisingly, another t-factor vehicle for aggressiveness. It can become a passive, nose-thumbing reproachfulness, a behavioral message which says, "You can't hope to get the better of me, so don't ever try."

Are you wasting your t-factor resources in time-killing maneuvers designed to stymie the authority figures in your life? If so, the chances are that up to now you haven't seen clearly the connection between the wasted time in your life and your feelings of anger and hostility toward others. It will be useful for you to trace your time-killing back to its aggressive roots and to deal with the aggression in a less self-destructive way.

T-Factor Juggling

The time-juggler represents the opposite extreme. He is acutely aware of time's scarcity and, in a form of natural-resource recycling, attempts to cram several activities into a time span that is generally restricted to just one. The teen-ager who does her homework at home, listens to a radio through an earphone in her right ear, talks on the telephone using the left ear, and keeps one eye on the television while polishing her toenails is a consummate time juggler. So is the business executive who presides over a meeting during which he jots down an agenda for the next meeting while pondering over what anniversary gift to buy his wife.

Is time-juggling an effective strategy for avoiding time waste? With certain exceptions, probably not. Our teen-ager's homework is probably riddled with errors and she is probably only dimly aware of the contents of the radio and television programs she is half attending to. The business executive probably has lost track of the session he's running, has omitted important items from the next meeting's agenda, and will end up purchasing a dreadful gift for his wife.

Both attempted to save time by handling individual tasks simultaneously, as if they were attempting to imitate sophisticated electronic computer systems which possess a built-in time-saving capability. In time-sharing a computer can perform several discrete computations simultaneously, by fitting one computation into the brief pauses that occur between other computations. The human brain, however, seems to lack this capacity to perform simultaneous operations efficiently, and so it's difficult to prevent one task from interfering with another. Research in delayed auditory feedback, for example, has shown that by playing back a person's spoken words through earphones with a few seconds' delay, his speech becomes thoroughly disrupted. He's unable to perform—simultaneously—the tasks of speaking and listening to his own words.

Successful time jugglers are the exceptional individuals who are *polychronic* as opposed to *monochronic*. These terms were applied by anthropologist Edward T. Hall to describe people who are truly capable of doing several things at once and those who are most comfortable doing one thing at a time.

Americans and Western Europeans are predominantly monochronic. Activities are scheduled one after another and we prefer to proceed step-by-step. Our t-factor is compartmentalized and fragmented into discrete, sequential units, as in television programming. We feel comfortable with television shows broken into half-hour, hour, and 90-minute parcels of time and resist the seemingly sensible notion that some programs might benefit from a viewing time of 83 minutes while others could usefully be trimmed to 16 minutes. Some experimental broadcasters attempted this flexible scheduling. Result: People stopped watching. They didn't know when to tune in and refused to master the complexities of programs that didn't run according to standard lengths.

Even our streets and highways seem designed to promote monochronism. Stores, homes, and sewers are laid out in linear fashion, one after another. Polychronic cultures in the Middle East and in the Latin nations of the Southern Hemisphere, offer a sharp contrast to monochronomity: congested plazas, markets, and galleries in which people, foods, and services are jumbled together for simultaneous use.

A business meeting between Middle Easterners, as Dr. Hall points out, may proceed without an agenda and may comfortably adjourn without ever touching upon the matter the meeting was supposedly concerned with. We might find such a meeting intolerable. In the same way, many children placed in open-classroom situations that lack rigid time structuring find themselves at a loss to handle this sort of learning setting. They yearn for the accustomed t-factor compartmentalization of the standard classroom.

When a person in our society attempts to juggle time, he or she is rubbing against the grain of deeply rooted cultural tendencies. True, the multiplicity of demands that modern life imposes on our limited store of the t-factor exerts powerful pressures on us to behave as though we were polychronic. But our monochronic nature and our accustomed behavior make it most difficult to become successful time jugglers. Only if you genuinely feel comfortably polychronic and only if your daily tasks bring you into contact with other polychronic individuals and activities can time-juggling become an effective strategy for conserving the t-factor in your life.

17

Putting the T-Factor to Work

While I've mostly been discussing how *not* to avoid the curse of wasted time, research also provides clues to positive time-saving strategies and t-factor efficiencies, methods for putting the t-factor to work.

One of the most important of these clues has been developed by psychologists interested in human learning, particularly the relationship between the t-factor and your ability to acquire new skills and abilities. Psychologists have long been aware of the central importance of the t-factor to learning. What, they have been wondering, is the most efficient way to allocate time to promote maximum learning?

Two basic t-factor approaches to learning have been investigated: massed learning and distributed learning. A learning psychologist has defined and contrasted these methods by asking "Is it better to practice a task with as little interruption for rest as possible, or is rest beneficial to learning and performance?"

Dr. Edward Litin attempted to answer this question by teaching groups of research subjects a difficult task, copying a design while looking at one's pencil and paper in a mirror. One group was offered massed learning: They performed the task 20 times without a pause. The other two groups were offered distributed learning: One received a minute's rest between drawings; the other received a day's rest. The results strongly supported the benefits of distributed practice. Those subjects who received a day's rest performed best, closely followed by those receiving a minute of rest. The poorest performances were turned in by those subjects who followed the massed approach. Other research confirmed this finding.

When you attempt to learn a new skill in preparing for an important challenge, you may be prone to cramming by massing your study within a short period in the belief that this works best. It should now be possible for you to switch to the more productive strategy of t-factor distribution and to set up brief study periods over a more extended time, and providing frequent short rest periods for yourself; this will increase your ability to acquire new skills and information.

Time psychology is also relevant to the problem-solving situations in your life. Psychologist Dr. Gary A. Davis has defined problem-solving as a "situation for which the organism does not have a ready response." It's a stop-and-think situation; you cannot merely choose between obvious alternatives. If you are wondering which cufflinks to wear this morning, this would hardly be a problem. But if you are away for the weekend and discover you've forgotten to bring cufflinks and all your shirts have buttonless cuffs, you have a genuine—if trivial—problem. Should you use paper clips to hold them together? Or string? Perhaps your wife's earrings would do.

When you are confronted with a problem for which you do not have a ready response, the multitude of memories contained within your psychological past cannot be of direct help to you. Your psychological past may even interfere with your problem-solving attempts. Psychologists have used the word *fixation* to describe the sort of t-factor interference with problem-solving abilities in which you become fixed into habitual patterns of thinking about, or handling, problems—patterns directed by your psychological past but inadequate to meet your present needs.

Dr. Martin Sheerer demonstrated how fixation may interfere with problem-solving by designing an experiment that required his test subjects to place rings over a peg six feet away from them. The subjects were provided two sticks three feet in length. There was also a string fastened by a nail to the experimental chamber's wall. Quickly, each subject solved the problem by removing the string, lashing the sticks together, and depositing the rings with the six-foot pole they had created to solve their problem.

But when Dr. Sheerer changed one simple detail of the experimental chamber—by hanging a NO SMOKING sign from the string on the wall—most subjects were at a loss to solve the problem. What they needed, many complained, was a nice piece of string. Due to fixation, they persisted in looking at the string on the wall as a permanent part of the NO SMOKING sign, not as a handy problem-solving tool. Nothing in their psychological pasts suggested to them that they might separate a string from a sign.

The Monkey Knows Best

T-factor fixation is not necessarily an indication of low or limited intelligence. A man and a monkey may both have an itch in an inaccessible, between-the-shoulder-blade region of their respective backs. Both may be holding a banana. The man is likely to peel the banana and eat it, musing over his itch. The monkey is likely to use the banana as a backscratcher and then eat it, solving two problems with one tool. The difference? To the man, a banana is exclusively a food. To the monkey, whose psychological past offers no such rigid fixations, a banana is a lengthy thing with several uses, among them, itch-removal.

If fixation is the villain of the psychological technique for problem-solving, defixation is the hero. To improve your problem-solving abilities, it seems necessary to cut through interference originating in your psychological past. One proven strategy for defixation is brainstorming. Developed by an advertising executive, Alex Osborn, this is an attempt to liberate your thinking from t-factor restraints by using "the principle of deferred judgment." This principle holds that an effective solution to a problem can be reached most effectively if your mind temporarily suspends its usual process of filtering thoughts through your psychological past.

Osborn suggests four ground rules for brainstorming. 1. Criticism is ruled out. Let your ideas flow unchecked. 2. Freewheeling is welcomed. Allow your ideas to roam untrammeled into unexpected directions. 3. Quantity is wanted. The more ideas, the better. 4. And most important, combination and improvement are sought. Once you've accumulated a large store of freewheeling ideas, let your psychological past re-enter the process, sifting, filtering, and rearranging these ideas until a useful combination is hit upon.

Another nontraditional t-factor approach to problem-solving and learning involves using that third of your daily allocation of 24 hours that is generally written off as wasted time: your nightly period of sleep. Some researchers have begun to wonder whether this time segment may be profitably put to work.

In one experiment a group of subjects was given a sequence of letters—*O,T,T,F,F*—before going to sleep. They were asked to provide the next two letters in the sequence upon awakening. Could they use their sleep time to solve this difficult problem?

Many of them did just that. One subject reported that she dreamed of walking down a street in search of a certain intersection. When she reached the corner of Sixth Avenue and Seventh Street she stopped. Another subject dreamed that he had gone to the race track and won $67. Other subjects reported dreams in which the number six and seven played important parts. They had solved the problem:

*O*ne, *T*wo, *T*hree, *F*our *F*ive, *S*ix, *S*even: *O,T,T,F,F,S,S*

Psychologists have also investigated the possibility of learning during sleep periods, a procedure called hyperopaedia. Sleep-learning has long been a staple of science fiction, its appeal resting in the attractive possibility that our nightly hours of unconsciousness may be retrieved for productive use.

Evidence exists that hyperopaedia may be possible. Two researchers at George Washington University, Drs. Bernard Fox and Joseph Robbin, performed a sleep learning experiment with 30 subjects. While ten of the subjects were asleep, a tape recording with a list of 25 Chinese words and their English translations was played. The second group heard music while asleep. The third group heard the same 25 Chinese words with incorrect translation. The next day each subject was tested to see how long it took him to learn the 25 words. The first group learned the words most quickly; the music group came in second; and the group that heard incorrect translation while asleep took about twice as long as the first group to learn the list. Clearly, sleep exposure to the correct words facilitated learning for the first group, while exposure to the incorrect words made it necessary for the third group to do some unlearning.

Other researchers have offered additional evidence that sleep-learning can be useful for t-factor conservation. There is some question whether a person actually learns while he is deeply asleep or whether he learns while he is in a drowsy state between sleep and wakefulness. There is little doubt, however, that our previously wasted nighttime hours may potentially be used more profitably. Currently, hyperopaedia remains an open question for psychological researchers interested in extracting the maximum benefits from the t-factor. If behavioral scientists are able to extend these early investigations into sleep-learning, your future may indeed offer the possibility of living on 24 hours a day.

18

Your Child and the T-Factor

Your child, no less than yourself, is confronted by a world full of time, but in many respects his experience of the t-factor differs from yours and forms a special province of childhood development. To help your child adopt a healthy relationship toward time, it will be useful for you to focus attention on the t-factor in childhood, to learn how your child's relationship to time grows and changes during the early years of life.

The Birth of Time

Some societies base a person's age on the estimated date of conception rather than the date of birth. In these cultures when a child is born he or she is considered to be approximately nine months old. This system seems more sensible than ours because it recognizes that an individual is affected to some extent by prenatal sensations and environmental influences.

One of the most important of these prenatal experiences is a primitive forerunner of time perception: rhythm. All through its gestation period, a developing fetus is exposed to the regular and rhythmic beating of a natural clock, the mother's heart. This is how the child-to-be begins to receive t-factor messages from the surrounding environment long before birth. The vague and diffuse thump-thump-thump of his mother's heartbeat is a familiar and perhaps comforting sound to the child by the time of birth.

This has prompted Dr. Lee Salk, a New York pediatric psychologist, to suggest that parents of a newborn infant who is having trouble falling asleep place a loudly ticking clock in the baby's crib. (Don't set the alarm!) The rhythmic beating of the clock, reminiscent of that old friend, mother's heartbeat, should comfort the child into drowsiness. In the same way, many old-fashioned baby-soothing strategies—rocking, cradling, walking the floor—are really attempts to recapture the rhythmic regularities of the maternal biological pacemaker. (One word of caution: At the moment this sentence is being written, the author's two-month-old daughter is crying vigorously, drowning out the stentorian tick of a trusty travel clock sitting beside her in the crib. Apparently she doesn't think much of modern child-rearing techniques.)

Although the infant seems to respond to rhythms and regularities on some primitive level, it has generally been presumed that the earliest months of life are pretty much characterized by timelessness, the infant remaining thoroughly divorced from the t-factor. Since infants cannot communicate their experiences to us, there is no way to confirm or refute this, but some researchers have speculated that the infant begins developing a rudimentary time frame right from the outset.

A team of researchers at New York University's Bellevue Medical Center, Drs. David Schecter, Martin Symonds, and Isidore Bernstein, has suggested that "premordial concepts of past, present, and future may develop in an infant." These time-frame concepts, they speculate, may arise when the infant becomes aware that events occur in regular sequences. The most important event for a newborn, of course, is hunger. He feels hungry, is fed, and feels satisfaction, a sequence that occurs and reoccurs as often as ten times a day in the earliest months. After a while, the infant may develop a primitive notion that feeding follows hunger and satisfaction follows feeding. As he is nursing, the infant may have a dim memory of his hunger in the immediate past. When he is hungry, he may anticipate the delivery of milk in the immediate future. And so the earliest time frame may be established.

Getting Acquainted with Time

If a new sort of Rosetta stone were to be discovered, enabling us to decipher the cries and babbles of babyhood, we would be able to test the merits of the infant time frame. Until this unlikely event occurs, the notion must remain plausible speculation. Studies of somewhat older children, however, have confirmed at least one element of the viewpoint; namely that a child's earliest ideas of time center completely on his bodily processes and functions. One of the earliest t-factor concepts that a child acquires, for example, is diurnal rhythm, the alternation between night and day. A three-year-old child, whose notions of time are closely connected to his bodily functions, will define the word day as something that begins "when I get out of bed," or "when I eat breakfast." Night, to the three-year-old, is "when I go to sleep."

A child who is eight years old bases his notions of night and day on external events rather than bodily functions. He defines day as "when the sun is in the sky" and night as "when it's dark outside." As the child is introduced to clock time, he begins to approximate an adult's notions of day and night.

An important t-factor notion that develops in childhood is that of age. The Swiss psychologist Jean Piaget has pointed out that young children frequently seem to confuse age with height or size. The bigger something is, to a four-year-old's mind, the older it is. A four-and-a-half-year-old girl, for example, whose mother happened to be three inches taller than her father, informed all visitors that "Mommy is much older than Daddy." And in a famous experiment, Piaget showed a group of 40 children ranging in age from four to ten years, pictures of a tall tree and a short one, asking "which tree is older?" A four-year-old insisted that the tall one was older. When Piaget asked, "Can't a tiny tree ever be older than a big one?" The child emphatically replied, "Oh no, no, no!" On the other hand, a seven-and-a-half-year-old replied quite sensibly, "Perhaps the tall one is the older one, but that's just a guess; one would have to know when they were planted."

Generally, Piaget found that children become able to separate the t-factor concept of age from the spatial concept of height at about the age of seven. And seven seems to be the critical age for a number of t-factor age concepts, including the idea that a person's age depends on the date he was born and a concept called conservation of age differences. This concept refers to the child's increasing awareness that differences between ages of people are constant, never growing or diminishing. If his mother is now 30 years older than he, you might ask a five-year-old: will his mother always be that much older than him? Schecter, Symonds, and Bernstein found that 75 percent of their five-year-old sample felt that age differences are not constant. They believed that they would someday "catch up" to a parent and attain equality of age. But in the six-year-old sample, the researchers found that only 16 percent still believed that they would be able to narrow the generation gap by catching up.

Piaget feels that it is the younger child's confusion between the notions of size and time that cause him to believe that he may overtake an adult's age. He points out that "we cannot see or perceive time as such since, unlike space or velocity, it does not impinge upon our senses." And because a young child's view of the world is completely shaped by his sensory experiences, it makes sense for him to adopt the pleasant supposition that an adult who has stopped growing taller has also stopped growing older. This explains the common phenomenon of a little girl extracting a promise from her favorite uncle that he will wait for her, so they can marry when she becomes as old as he is. The adult may dismiss these wishes as a cute childish fantasy; actually, the girl is communicating her natural perspective on the t-factor.

Piaget has discovered that a young child bases his sense of duration as well as age on size and distance. In a typical experiment, Piaget would make a child watch two toy cars, a fast one and a slow one, start from the same point and run a distance of two feet. Although the slow car actually took twice as long to cover the distance as the fast one, the four- or five-year-old will say they both ran for the same amount of time. Conversely, if a slow toy car took 20 seconds to run one foot while a fast car covered two feet in 10 seconds, the child will say that the fast car had been traveling longer. In both cases, the child judges time completely according to the evidence of his senses, equating how long with how far. By the age of seven or eight, the child's abstract abilities have developed to the point where he can conceive of an invisible concept like time as something separate from a visible idea like distance.

In an interesting parallel to our Chapter 3 exploration of your psychological week, Dr. Schecter's research team asked its sample of three-to-six-year-olds to describe what each day of the week meant to them. Obviously, as a child grows older, his sphere of activities expands and his psychological week becomes more meaningful. The three- and four-year-old nursery-school children, for example, were uniformly unable to describe the midweek days of Tuesday, Wednesday, and Thursday. They described Monday as the day to "start school." Saturday is a "no school" day. Sunday is "play with daddy" or "watch TV" day, and Friday is "no nap" day. The five- and six-year-olds were able to describe each day more distinctly. Monday "school begins," Tuesday "gym," Wednesday "ice-skating," Thursday "music," Friday "ice-skating," Saturday "no school," and Sunday "visiting."

One of the most important implications of these descriptions of the week is that the children tend to view each day in terms of its personal significance. An adult might call Wednesday "the midweek part," but a child prefers to describe it as "ice-skating day." Similarly, in handling the concepts of age, past, present, future, and duration, children again seem to filter their notions of time through the sieve of their uniquely personal experiences.

It's fair to say, therefore, during childhood a person is most intimately involved with time as he or she experiences it. With maturation and development of the ability to handle time as an abstract idea, their highly personalized view of time recedes into the background and finally fades away. Isn't it ironic that the attempt to understand the t-factor in your life as an adult —time as you personally experience it—requires that you recapture to some degree the personalized relationship with time that you outgrew during childhood?

Your Child's T-Factor and Learning

Psychologists have long been fascinated by the vast intellectual differences they observe between children. Many explanations for these differences have been offered, ranging from genetically built-in ability levels and differences in home environments to the quality of educational experiences. While not disputing the significance of these forces, a Harvard University psychologist, Jerome Kagan, has suggested that the t-factor may also play an important role.

Dr. Kagan feels that children may differ in conceptual tempo and describes some as reflective and others as impulsive. A reflective child, when confronted by a problem with several possible solutions, is able to carefully consider each solution and then to produce an answer. An impulsive child says the first thing that comes into his mind. In one item of a test called Matching Familiar Figures, the child is shown a picture of a teddy bear sitting on a chair. Below it are six similar pictures, but only one matches the first picture exactly. The child's task is to identify the exactly matching picture.

Dr. Kagan found that some children, the impulsive ones,

tended to produce a response almost immediately, while others, the reflectives, delayed responding. When each child's accuracy was compared to his speed of response, it became clear that the impulsive children had made many more errors than the reflective children. More significantly, Dr. Kagan found little relationship between a child's verbal abilities and his score in the test. So the t-factor variable of reflectivity versus impulsivity accounted almost entirely for the differences between these children.

These findings have important implications for your attempts to help your child develop a productive relationship to the t-factor. While Dr. Kagan believes that some children may have an impulsive conceptual tempo because of built-in biological reasons, he feels that factors found in the child's environment are also crucial in determining a child's impulsivity or reflectivity.

One such factor is task involvement. If a child sets high standards of performance for himself and cares about the quality of his work, he will tend to become more reflective and to make fewer impulsive errors. A second factor relates to the attitudes a child picks up from the adults around him. Typically, Dr. Kagan points out, a child receives two conflicting meanings from parents and teachers: work quickly and don't make mistakes. Of course, these messages operate at cross-purposes. If he works too quickly, he is bound to make mistakes. Armed with this information you are in a position to help your child deal more prudently with the t-factor. By promoting task-involvement and reducing your stress upon speed at the expense of accuracy, you will be able to assist your child developing a valuable, reflective t-factor approach to his learning experiences.

The T-Factor Gap

If your child's experience of time differs so markedly from yours, it should come as no surprise that a similar gulf separates his attitudes toward the t-factor from your own. This t-factor gap is partially the result of biological differences between adults and children and partly due to more purely mental factors.

On the biological level, a child's bodily rhythms are set at a considerably faster rate than those of an adult. In modern hospital maternity wings, for example, a mother in labor is routinely hooked up to a fetal heartbeat monitor. This device detects the rhythm of the fetal heart, producing an audible blip for each fetal beat. Many women are surprised at the rapidity of the fetal heartbeat and express concern because the blips come at such a rapid-fire pace. Doctors are quick to offer assurance, explaining that an infant's heartbeat is normally much speedier than an adult's.

A young child's sleep and dream patterns reveal a similar acceleration in biological rhythms. While an adult has been found to have, on average, one dream for each 90 minutes of sleep, newborns pursue a double-time dream cycle, dreaming once for each 40 to 50 minutes of sleep. Correspondingly, babies spend a greater proportion of their sleep time engaged in making rapid eye movement, the quick back-and-forth motions of their closed eyes which occur during dream states. At birth, a baby may spend up to 85 percent of his sleep time in the active REM state; an adult's sleep behavior is much less dynamic.

Generally, children enter the world resembling biological clocks with tightly wound mainsprings. Early life races along by swift biological rhythms that gradually decelerate, leveling off at an even adult rate for several decades, and then decelerating once more during the years of late adulthood. Since the biological pacemaker of childhood is set at this extremely rigid level, it would be reasonable to expect differences between children and adults in t-factor attitudes.

Nowhere is this t-factor gap more striking than in the relationship between a child and a grandparent. To a child, time seems literally endless. To some extent, of course, this feeling results from the child's common sense realization that most of his life lies ahead. But a more comprehensive explanation recognizes that the child's biological pacemaker is set at so rapid a level that his internal time sense races in comparison to clock time, which is why clock time seems to pass very slowly for the child. After school lets out in June, a small child's two-month summer vacation will seem to take two years to pass by.

For the child's grandparent, the situation is reversed. The grandparent's biological pacemaker has decelerated; his internal time sense is slowed in comparison to clock time, which therefore seems to be racing by at a headlong pace. To the grandparent, time is a rapidly vanishing commodity; it feels precisely the opposite of endless. When a grandparent admonishes a child to "make the most of every day because life is short," he should not be startled to receive a puzzled "huh?" in response. The child's t-factor attitude, arising from his rapid biological pacemaker is diametrically opposed to that of the grandparent.

To a somewhat lesser, but still significant extent, there is a t-factor gap between parents and children. Take the rainy day blues. Few parents have been spared the experience of spending a housebound day with a bored child who complains "there's nothing to do." What a parent usually does not realize is that the child's boredom springs in large part from his accelerated biological pacemaker. The hours from noon to six on a rainy Saturday seem, to a child, like an endless tract of time, impossible to fill with enjoyable activities.

In Chapter 9, I discussed why complicated or difficult experiences seem to last longer than simple or easy-to-code experiences. This enables us to understand more clearly a child's feeling that time is slow-moving and endless. Since the child is continually confronted by the complexities of a confining, hard to understand environment, his experiences are almost constantly complex, difficult to code and require considerable psychological work. In response to this state of affairs, his mental pacemaker decelerates and leads him to feel that time is passing slowly. He is driving his time machine through unfamiliar territory; to understand the landscape he must naturally proceed at reduced speed. But his parent has mastered much of the environment; so, like a seasoned navigator, he is able to drive his time machine at a faster rate.

One important repercussion of this attitude gap is a tendency on the part of parents to romanticize, and sometimes envy, the seemingly endless time of childhood. In a classic paper titled "Time and the Unconscious," the psychoanalyst Marie Bonaparte delineated this attitude, remarking, "Children wake from their slumbers, get up, run about, eat, play, laugh, and cry in a time whose sweep is of a very different order from that of the brief, pathetic time engaged by adults."

But children rarely share their parents' romantic notions about the t-factor in childhood. While a parent may feel a pang on seeing his child strap on his first wristwatch—which the parent may regard as a handcuff, imprisoning the child within a world of schedules—a child finds this attitude incomprehensible. Rather than viewing the end of childhood as pathetic, a child is likely to regard it as extremely desirable: It spells liberation from a seemingly endless period of dependency and limited freedom.

What Children Need to Learn About Time

Dr. Franklin S. DuBois has defined an emotionally healthy adult as one who "experiences the present harmoniously as a bridge between a pleasant past and a hopeful future with its opportunities for accomplishment." The major t-factor task of childhood, then, is the construction of a pleasant psychological past and a hopeful psychological future. How can you help your child establish such a time frame?

The crucial ingredient is the development of a feeling of competence, a sense of mastery over the environment. Child-

hood experiences of effectiveness are stored in the psychological past and serve as capital for the psychological future. Dr.
Martin Seligman, whom I mentioned in explaining the depressive time trap, suggests that children be trained to live "the
masterful life."

A youngster's success experiences, according to Dr. Seligman and other scientists, tend to enhance his concept of himself, to enable him to meet future challenges with a sense of
power and control over his own destiny. A parent can assist his
child's entry into the masterful life by exposing him to challenges consistent with his abilities. A poorly coordinated child,
obviously, is likely to acquire a strong sense of failure if his
parents convey the expectation that he excel in competitive
athletics. But by teaching him a noncompetitive skill—swim-
ming, for example—his parent will build an experience of
mastering into the child's psychological past. An academically
average child, in the same way, will accumulate a debilitating
collection of self-doubts in his psychological past if his parents insist upon prodigies of intellectual performance. But he
will bloom with self-confidence if he is enabled to succeed in
living up to his unique potential.

Primarily, then, the parent's t-factor task centers on a realistic approach toward his child's capacities and a consistent
attempt to promote success and mastering of experiences. In
this way, the child may come to confront his psychological
future confidently and hopefully, enjoying a firm footing in the
psychological past.

19

Steering Your Time Machine Into the Future

How will you experience time in the future—your future?

Let's begin with another question: Where is your future? Where is it located? If you picture time as a highway, do you visualize your future as a stretch of the road extending far ahead into the distance? Or do you see your future located around the bend from the present, hidden by a curve in time's highway, but nevertheless ahead of you?

Most of us do visualize the future in these terms; a young person feels that his life is ahead of him, while an elderly person may lament the fact that her life is all behind her. Similarly, by drawing your time frame as a left-to-right progression from the past through the present into the future, we automatically adopted the notion that the future lies ahead in space as well as time. In all of these ways, we see ourselves constantly moving forward into the future, the headlights of our time machine casting exploratory beams into the mysterious darkness that awaits down the highway of time.

But it is possible—and instructive—to consider an alternate location of the future, an attitude that may free us from habitual patterns of thinking and speaking. Consider, for example, the way a Peruvian Indian tribe, the Quechua, thinks about the future. According to anthropologist Peter Farb, a Quechua Indian "thinks of the future as being 'behind oneself' and the past as being 'ahead of one.' He very logically states that past events can be seen in the mind since they already happened, and therefore they must be in front of his eyes. But since he can't 'see' into the future, these events must therefore be out of sight or 'behind' him."

Looking at the t-factor through the eyes of a Quechua Indian, we are offered the tantalizing possibility that we might not be advancing at all, either boldly or timidly, into the future. We may actually be backing into the future, our eyes firmly fixed on the past as we leave it receding from us. We might compare the Quechua's attitude toward the future to our own experience of driving a car in reverse gear. If we look only through the front windshield, all we see is where we have been—not where we are heading. While this is an extremely hazardous driving technique, we can glance into the rearview mirror and catch a picture—admittedly narrow and limited—of what lies in the path of our backwardly advancing automobile.

So we can combine the Quechua's picture of the future with our own viewpoint to arrive at a useful perspective of time as you will experience it. In this perspective, your time machine is indeed backing into the future while the past recedes before your eyes. But it is not necessary for you to back blindly into the future. Your time machine is equipped with a rearview mirror enabling you to steer a tentative course. Your task is to make maximum use of the mirror, to steer the best possible course into the future. Let us see what the mirror reveals and how to make the most of its revelations.

How Proactive Are You?

By thinking about the future in this unconventional way, we raise a revealing question: How much do you actually choose to look into the mirror? Some of us look through the mirror infrequently or not at all; others subject the mirror to steady scrutiny.

Dr. Hubert Bonner, a psychologist at Ohio Wesleyan University, has contrasted these two styles of dealing with the future. He calls the former style reactive and the latter proactive. The reactive individual is a person who rarely chooses to gaze into the future-facing mirror. He is a creature of his own past. Everything he does is based on previous experience; he does not *plan* to imitate his earlier behavior; he merely reacts to the contents of his psychological past. Essentially, he is backing blindly into the future. He assumes that the unseen road behind him is no different from the familiar road that he sees slipping away through his windshield.

The proactive individual is pulled by the future, rather than pushed by the past. He concentrates intently on the future-facing mirror and wants an active role in the shaping of his future, not a passive, reactive role. As Dr. Bronner says: "The healthy, creative individual lives in the process of becoming, and this requires a future for its actualization. . . . He is a seeker of future ends."

So your ability to steer your time machine into the future depends strongly on your proactivity or reactivity. If you are totally proactive and choose never to gaze into the future-facing mirror, the success of your steering will rest on the frail hope that your future will be an exact mirror image of your past.

It is interesting that we use the term *reactionary* to describe someone who seeks to repeat the past in the future. If he could accomplish this, he would remove the peril from his reactive refusal to look into the future. If you are totally proactive and focus your complete attention on the future-facing mirror, you will steer more effectively but pay a price for this effectiveness: the absence of roots and the lack of a sense of belongingness and tradition in your life.

A balance between reactivity and proactivity is therefore

desirable, with your gaze alternating between the future-facing mirror and the window to the past. Usually this balance will be achieved through an increase in proactivity, since most of us—as I will show in the not too distant future—tend to avoid looking into the future-facing mirror.

Your best first step in steering your time machine into the future, therefore, is to assess the dominant trend in your approach to the future—reactive vs. proactive—and to bring these forces into a balance so you can see where you are going as well as where you have been.

The Size of Your Future

How much of your future is visible through your time-machine's future-facing mirror? Is it only a narrow slice of time's highway? Or a broad segment of time stretching into the far distance? These are the next major questions that must be answered to help you steer your time machine into the future, and they have been thoroughly investigated by time psychologists who study *temporal perspective*.

Temporal perspective is your perception of the psychological size of the various parts of your time frames. To some of us, the psychological future seems to occupy the bulk of the time frame, dwarfing in size the psychological past and present; for others, the future occupies but a narrow slice on the time frame. These differences in temporal perspective must be taken into account when you examine your own unique problems of navigating into the future. As Harvard time psychologist Dr. Thomas J. Cottle put it: "Can one meaningfully discuss a future orientation . . . if for some the future commences seconds from now, while for others an expanse literally of years appertains to what they themselves call present?"

The answer, of course, is no. To discuss your future orientation meaningfully you will find it helpful first to get some idea of your future time perspective, the size of your psychological future.

One simple method is to make two lists in the columns provided below. In the column labeled PAST, list the first ten events you think of that you experienced in the past. In the column labeled FUTURE, list ten events that you expect will occur in the future.

Now, next to each item in the PAST column, beneath the heading H.L.A? (short for How Long Ago?), note how many years have passed since each event occurred. And beneath the heading H.L.F.N? (How Long From Now?), estimate how many years you expect to pass before each FUTURE event takes place.

PAST	H.L.A?	FUTURE	H.L.F.N?
1. _____	_____	1. _____	_____
2. _____	_____	2. _____	_____
3. _____	_____	3. _____	_____
4. _____	_____	4. _____	_____
5. _____	_____	5. _____	_____
6. _____	_____	6. _____	_____
7. _____	_____	7. _____	_____
8. _____	_____	8. _____	_____
9. _____	_____	9. _____	_____
10. _____	_____	10. _____	_____
	SUM = _____		SUM = _____
	SUM/10 = _____		SUM/10 = _____

Once you have filled in all the columns, add up your ten H.L.A? estimates and your ten H.L.F.N? estimates. When you divide each of these sums by ten, you will wind up with a reasonably accurate estimate of the relative sizes of your psychological past and psychological future. You may learn, for instance, that your psychological future occupies a broad 20-year swath of your time frame, while your psychological past is crammed, on average, into a 5-year slice. Or you may find the reverse.

Judging from the results of research, you are most likely to discover that the size of your psychological future matches the size of your psychological past almost precisely. This was the finding of Dr. T. D. Graves who, as a graduate student at the University of Pennsylvania, used this method to investigate the temporal perspectives of 133 high school students. He found a high correlation between the size of each student's psychological future and the size of his past. The more remote were the listed events of the past, the further into the future each student would estimate each anticipated event to lie.

Other researchers confirmed this discovery, as perhaps you have just done yourself. But why should the size of your psychological future be so closely linked to the size of your psychological past?

Some psychologists believe that the ability to anticipate future events is closely related to the capacity to remember and organize past experiences. Which is why people with broad, well-organized psychological pasts would be expected also to possess extensive and detailed navigational maps of the psychological future.

Perhaps the best analogy to account for the link between past size and future size is a tree and its roots. The taller a tree, the deeper its roots sink into the earth. In the same way, the more deeply rooted you are in the soil of your psychological past, the taller the tree of your psychological future is likely to be. And just as a small tree has short roots, people with a shallow psychological past are likely to have a short psychological future.

Another way to think about the size of your psychological future is to wonder exactly where your psychological present ends and where your future begins. Dr. Cottle asked 332 men and 98 women to complete the following sentence:

"The distant future, as I think of it, includes things and events which will occur _____ from now, while the near future includes things and events which will occur _____ from now."

The subjects were instructed to use one of the following seven words to fill each blank space:

1. Seconds
2. Minutes
3. Hours
4. Days
5. Weeks
6. Months
7. Years

By completing these sentences, you will obtain a notion of the borderline that separates your own psychological present from your psychological future. The higher the numbers of the words you select, the more extensive is the border between your psychological present and your psychological future, and the longer you feel it will take you to enter the future sector of your time frame. For example, if you inserted the word *months* (6) into the second blank space and the word *years* (7) into the first, the border between your present and future is broader than that of a person who inserted the words *seconds* (1) and *minutes* (2) into those spaces.

It is interesting that men and women seem to differ in where they place the borderline between present and future. Dr. Cottle found that the women he studied tended to view the future as further away from the present than did his sample of men. His female subjects also regarded the past as being further back in time from the present than did the males.

It may be that our society has traditionally assigned males the role of planning for the future and females the role of tending to the present. These sex differences would explain the research findings, since the males viewed the future as closer to them, while the females regarded the present as a longer lasting span of time. If male and female members of a later generation, which faces less sex-role stereotyping, are asked to perform this psychological test, it is likely that these male–female t-factor differences will have evaporated.

Your Family and the Future

The generations themselves, particularly generations within families, are also crucial ingredients in shaping how you will experience time in the future. Are generational boundaries proliferating, as some suggest, so that a 30-year-old man and his 27-year-old sister represent two different generations? Or is the opposite process unfolding, with the boundaries between generations disappearing so that a 20-year-old and his 80-year-old grandmother may be, in a psychologically significant sense, tuned into the same generational wavelength?

Common sense seems to support the view that the generations are multiplying. The pace of social change has become so rapid that the psychological past of a 15-year-old in 1967 was quite different from that of a person who became 15 in 1971. As a matter of fact, some social theorists regard generational multiplication as the necessary result of a lack of shared past experiences between individuals who are relatively close to each other in age. In past-oriented societies that transmit rituals and traditions from one generation to the next there is no tendency toward quickly changing generations. Members of such societies share a collective psychological past which retards change.

As members of our own society have become increasingly distrustful of tradition and therefore less and less able to guide their actions, feelings, and beliefs in accordance with a shared sense of the psychological past, each narrowly defined age group established its own values, symbols, and traditions—all of them oriented largely toward the present. Time psychologists Thomas Cottle and Steven Klineberg have pointed out that "As the past grows increasingly remote and discontinuous with the present, the future, too, is likely to be conceived as unpredictable, its images unsafe as guides for current actions and meanings."

So it is not surprising that today's 21-year-olds differ considerably from today's 24-year-olds. Each age group has responded to the remoteness of the psychological past and the unpredictability of the psychological future by becoming rooted in a psychological present that bears little relationship to that of other age groups.

But perhaps the differences between each of these mini-generations is a matter more of style than of substance. Some investigators have wondered whether a broad continuity stretches beneath the beards and Levi's of the younger generation and the teased hair and neckties of the older. Their research suggests that the family may actually function as an anti-time machine, blurring the seemingly sharp and apparently multiplying distortions between the generations.

One indication that the family is a powerful source of intergenerational stability was found in voting patterns when the voting age was lowered to 18. Politicians eager to exploit the youth vote discovered that there was really only one relatively sure-fire way to predict which party a young person was likely to support: his parents' political affiliation.

On a deeper psychological level, Drs. Seymour Fisher and David Mendell have gathered research data that demonstrates that patterns of emotion and thoughts do not seem to differ between succeeding generations of the same family. The researchers studied 6 three-generation families, which included grandparents, parents, and children, and 14 two-generation families consisting of parents and children. Dr. Mendell, a psychiatrist, interviewed members of each family; Dr. Fisher, a psychologist, obtained psychological test information from each family member.

The psychological test material was examined blindly; that is, names were removed from each person's test responses. The researchers then attempted to group the tests into family clusters, using only psychological similarities between the responses of the unidentified individuals as a guide. Drs. Fisher and Mendell found that certain tests did show striking similarities. When names were put back on the tests, the researchers discovered that they had indeed been successful in grouping together members of families spanning several generations, based only on psychological commonalities between the family members.

For example, in a family consisting of a mother, father, son, and maternal grandmother, the mother's psychological test responses centered strongly about concerns with cleanliness and a preoccupation with being dirty. Her son's responses were quite similar; to one Rorschach inkblot he responded that it looked like "people covered with soapsuds." Her husband described another Rorschach blot as resembling "messy" scraps of meat. The grandmother described a picture as looking like "a pipe leaking dirty water."

The researchers found many such instances of powerful similarities on a deep psychological level between members of a family representing several generations. They suggested that "each family tends to be characterized by a special 'flavor' or 'atmosphere,' " a psychological bond which reaches across and dissolves generational boundaries. So while it may be that members of succeeding generations—and even older and younger members of the same generation—display important contrasts in values, attitudes, and actions, it is just as useful for you to remember that family patterns of thinking and feeling will follow you from the past into the future.

How to Scan the Future

Earlier we explored the significance that anticipation holds for the psychological future section of your time frame and later we examined how anticipation may lead you into a time trap. Yet another aspect of anticipation strangely affects your ability to steer your time machine into the future: prediction.

Prediction is your most important tool for navigating through the mists of your psychological future. We all make innumerable predictions each day. We predict that an approaching automobile will stop at a red light, permitting us to cross the street safely. We see clouds in the sky, predict that it will rain, and remember to take an umbrella to work. We buy a book by a favorite author because his track record predicts that it will be enjoyable to read.

We also make extremely serious predictions. Early in life, we predict that a certain occupation will be fulfilling and select a career based on the prediction. We predict that a certain individual will provide decades of love and mutual admiration, and we base the decision to marry on that prediction. We predict that a company will increase its earning and decide to invest money or purchase stock in the company.

In short, much of your future-oriented planning is based on your ability to predict. But prediction is a hazardous enterprise, a bet that anyone who finds himself trapped in a dull job, an unpleasant marriage, or a bankrupt investment will confirm. Fortunately, there are methods to improve the quality of your predictions and enable you to create accurate maps of your psychological future. These methods help you prevent making common errors in prediction, errors which psychologist Carole Wade Offir has called "psychological screens that make us see the future dimly."

Dr. Offir has identified a number of such navigational hazards, and three seem particularly important. The first is called the gambler's fallacy and relates to your grasp of the law of averages. If you toss a coin nine times, for example, and obtain nine heads in a row, what are the odds that the coin will turn up tails on the next toss? Ninety percent?

No, the odds are precisely 50–50 that each toss of the coin will turn up tails, regardless of how many or how few times it did so in the past. In the long run, tails and heads all balance, but the odds don't change for any particular toss. This psychological principle is of major importance for your ability to predict the future.

When you feel that you have been having a run of bad luck in your life, the gambler's fallacy may lead you to predict that any decision you make next is likely to turn out favorably. It therefore becomes important to base your predictions on more solid foundations than the fickle law of averages.

Dr. Offir calls her second predictive screen faith in small numbers—the tendency to let reason leap from a part to a whole. A blind man, legend has it, touched an elephant's trunk and decided that the creature mostly resembled a horse. A second blind man, touching the elephant's leg, predicted that the animal really looked like the stump of a tree. Each was basing his prediction of the whole creature on one unrepresentative part.

Your own predictions may suffer from a similar fallacy. If you dislike a person at first glance and, predicting that you and he will never become friends, you decide against any further involvement, you may be foreclosing yourself from a most rewarding relationship. Your poor decision could have been avoided by a larger number of observations. And if you take a job on the basis of a casual inspection of its duties, you may live to regret a prediction resting on so narrow a base.

A third predictive screen described by Dr. Offir is called the availability trap, and relates to our common tendency to restrict predictions to those outcomes that are the most available in our imaginations. For example, some people who are required to make a choice between hiring a male lawyer and a female lawyer will automatically opt for the male, regardless of each lawyer's relative merits, experience, and qualifications. These decision-makers are not necessarily sexists. The image of a lawyer as a male is just more available to their minds than the picture of a woman attorney and therefore tends to channel their prediction into a possibly mistaken choice. This predictive screen, then, is similar to the fixation barrier to problem-solving explained in Chapter 18. Your ability to lower this screen rests on your willingness to examine future alternatives flexibly.

I have been discussing prediction as though we agreed that it is a completely desirable skill to possess and that all of us wish to be able to steer ourselves into the future equipped with navigational maps that are as accurate as possible. Perhaps this is not an entirely safe assumption. Suppose you were offered a free medical examination and the results inform you of the precise date of your death, would you really want this information? Would you wish to remove the mystery from your psychological future?

Probably not. Research by Dr. Thomas Cottle, using a questionnaire called the Future Commitment Scale discovered that people are not particularly willing to gaze into the future-facing mirror. His scale consisted of 31 statements about future events. Some were personal—My children will become pretty successful—and some were impersonal—Russia and America will live in peaceful coexistence. The research subjects were asked to label each statement True, False, or Can't Say.

Dr. Cottle found that men and women both tended strongly to respond with Can't Say to statements connected to the personal future, although many were quite willing to answer either True or False to impersonal statements. So it seems likely that the most important predictive screen may not be your faith in small numbers or the availability trap. Rather, it may be your own natural reluctance to look into the future, which you might do well to overcome if you want to get the most out of the time ahead.

What You Can Do About Time

Our exploration of the t-factor in your life is coming to an end—and, hopefully, a beginning.

Stored loosely in your psychological past, already undergoing the processes of sharpening and leveling, is a harvest of time psychology's most fruitful findings, facts, and scientifically sound fantasies. From the activity of your biomental pacemaker to the development of t-factor awareness in your children, from time traps through time bombs to time distortions, our attention has been consistently focused on one central concern: the t-factor in your life, time as you experience it.

Perhaps the most important lesson to be learned from time psychology is that each of your actions, feelings, and thoughts is affected in a great variety of ways by the atmosphere of time that surrounds your life. Equipped with the tools of time psychology, you are now in a better position to understand, predict, and, in some degree, control the impact that the t-factor will exert on you during the days and years to come.

For time is in a real sense the very fabric of your life and the raw material of your existence. Your task is to shape the t-factor into forms that are productive and useful to you. Then you can make the t-factor your servant rather than your master and steer your time machine confidently into the future.

Have a good journey.